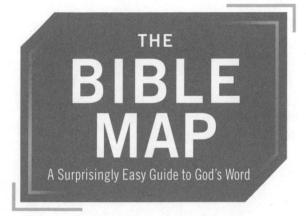

THE
BIBLE
MAP

A Surprisingly Easy Guide to God's Word

TRACY M. SUMNER

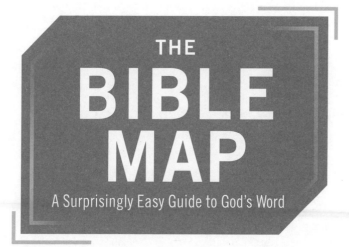

THE
BIBLE
MAP

A Surprisingly Easy Guide to God's Word

BARBOUR
PUBLISHING

ISBN 978-1-63609-577-6

Published by Barbour Publishing, Inc., 1810 Barbour Drive, Uhrichsville, Ohio 44683, www.barbourbooks.com

Our mission is to inspire the world with the life-changing message of the Bible.

Printed in China.

CONTENTS

Welcome to THE SEVEN "LANDS" OF THE BIBLE

When you want to explore the Bible, you'll need a map. That's what this surprisingly easy guide to God's Word is all about.

The Bible Map will walk you through seven distinct "lands" of scripture:

- ▶ **Origins**: where everything comes from
- ▶ **Sin**: the problem that affects everyone
- ▶ **God's People**: Israel as a blessing to all nations
- ▶ **Exile**: the sin and decline of God's people
- ▶ **the Messiah**: Jesus' life and teaching, death and resurrection
- ▶ **Christianity**: the birth and growth of the church
- ▶ **the End Times**: Jesus' return and the renewal of all things

The "main road" of the Bible features highlights of God's Word in chronological order. These passage-by-passage summaries are explained within the overarching theme of God's love for humanity. Meanwhile, "side roads"—curious and confusing elements of scripture—are also explored. For example, when you understand the three different types of Old Testament law, you'll see why many Christians today eat pork and shellfish when the ancient Israelites could not.

Ultimately, *The Bible Map* directs you to the God who made you, loves you, and longs for you to be part of His family. Read on for a potentially life-changing journey through scripture!

1. ORIGINS:
Where Everything Comes From

God Creates the Universe and the Earth (Genesis 1:1–10, 14–19)

The book of Genesis, the very first book of the Bible, begins with the words, "In the beginning God created the heaven and the earth." On that first of six creation days, God made the earth (and the whole universe) out of nothing. But our world looked nothing like it later would.

Genesis 1:2 says, "The earth was without form and void. And darkness was on the face of the deep." Our world wasn't yet ready for humans—or any other living creatures. But over the next five days, God fashioned this world into a version that was a perfect place for human life.

God Creates Life (Genesis 1:11–13, 20–31)

On the first creation day (Genesis 1:1–5), God made the heavens and the earth, as well as light. He created the sky (our atmosphere) on day 2 (verses 6–8). On day 3 (verses 9–13), God fashioned dry land and made the first living things—plants. On day 4 (verses 14–19) He created the sun, moon, and stars. On day 5 (verses 20–23) God introduced both water-dwelling creatures and birds to the earth. And on day 6 (verses 24–31) He created everything that lives on dry land, including human beings.

Where Did God Come From?

The Bible starts with the familiar words "In the beginning God created. . ." This means everything He made had a beginning, and is therefore finite. But what about God? Where did He come from?

The Bible says nothing about God having any kind of beginning. In fact, Moses, the man credited with writing Genesis (as well as the second through fifth books of the Bible), said, "Before the mountains were brought forth or You had ever formed the earth and the world, even from everlasting to everlasting, You are God" (Psalm 90:2).

While God's creation came from somewhere, God Himself had no beginning—He's simply always been. God's own name for Himself reflects this self-existent, eternal nature: "I AM THAT I AM" (Exodus 3:14).

The concept of an all-knowing, all-powerful, eternally self-existent God is far beyond our finite human comprehension. But that is the reality of who He is.

God Creates Humanity (Genesis 1:26–30, 2:21–25)

On the first five days of creation, God showed both His infinite power and His amazing creativity. But when He formed His most prized creation—human beings—He demonstrated His love. God spent the majority of creation week preparing the world, waiting until the sixth day to fashion a living being who could relate to Him in a loving, personal way—in much the same way a child relates to its loving parent.

On that sixth day of creation, God used the simple dirt He'd already created to form the first man, called Adam. Then, from Adam's own body, God created a complementary partner named Eve. God blessed them both and said, "Be fruitful and multiply, and replenish the earth, and subdue it. And have dominion over the fish of the sea and over the fowl of the air and over every living thing that moves on the earth" (Genesis 1:28).

In His Image (Genesis 1:26–27)

God created every living thing on the earth, but we humans are the only ones made in His own image. We are not all-knowing and all-powerful, of course, but we reflect God's nature and character in many important ways. For example, we have the ability to reason and communicate like He does. Human beings were also created to rule over the earth and all the other living things God put here.

The Bible says that God "breathed into [Adam's] nostrils the breath of life, and man became a living soul" (Genesis 2:7). At that point, Adam gained not just physical life but a spirit and soul. He possessed the ability to do something none of the animals could: communicate with God in a personal, loving way.

Where Was the Garden of Eden?

"The LORD God planted a garden eastward in Eden, and there He put the man whom He had formed. And out of the ground the LORD God made to grow every tree that is pleasant to the sight and good for food. The tree of life was also in the midst of the garden, and the tree of knowledge of good and evil" (Genesis 2:8–9).

The garden of Eden was likely a beautiful place that produced plenty of good food for Adam and Eve and their offspring. Though the Bible never offers an exact location, it does say that "a river went out of Eden to water the garden, and from there it parted and became four heads. The name of the first is Pishon; it is the one that compasses the whole land of Havilah, where there is gold. . . . And the name of the second river is Gihon; it is the same one that surrounds the whole land of Ethiopia. And the name of the third river is Hiddekel; it is the one that goes toward the east of Assyria. And the fourth river is Euphrates" (Genesis 2:10–14).

The Pishon and Gihon rivers have been lost to history, but the Hiddekel, also called the Tigris, and Euphrates both flow to this day. If these latter waterways mentioned in Genesis are the same as the two modern rivers, then the garden of Eden would have been located somewhere in the Middle East, probably Iraq.

God Creates Marriage (Genesis 2:18–24)

Before God created Eve, He had placed Adam in the garden of Eden and commanded him to take care of it (Genesis 2:15). But God knew something was missing: Every other creature in the garden had a mate, because God had made both male and female of each species. But that was not yet the case with human beings.

God said to Himself, "It is not good that the man should be alone; I will make him a help suitable for him" (Genesis 2:18). So God put Adam into deep sleep, then took a rib from his side. From this, God created Eve to be Adam's wife.

Adam seemingly loved what he saw when he first laid eyes on Eve. "This is now bone of my bones and flesh of my flesh," he exclaimed. "She shall be called Woman, because she was taken out of Man" (Genesis 2:23). It became a union that prefigured every marriage to follow: "Therefore a man shall leave his father and his mother and shall cleave to his wife, and they shall be one flesh" (Genesis 2:24).

God Rests (Genesis 2:1–3)

Much of Genesis 2 is a more detailed revisiting of the creation of human beings. But the first three verses of the chapter provide a wrap-up of creation week, by noting that "God ended His work that He had made, and He rested on the seventh day from all His work that He had made" (Genesis 2:2).

The next verse notes that "God blessed the seventh day and sanctified it, because in it He had rested from all His work that God created and made" (Genesis 2:3). God didn't need to rest from weariness; He simply stopped His creative efforts. His example set apart one day of rest from each seven-day week. Many years later, God made that day of rest a law for His chosen people, the Israelites (Exodus 20:8–11).

How Does the Creation Account of Genesis 2 Align with Genesis 1?

Genesis 1 and Genesis 2 tell complementary creation stories. Genesis 1 gives the account of all six creation days, while Genesis 2 covers just the creation of humankind in greater detail.

Some skeptics argue there are two contradictions between Genesis 1 and Genesis 2—the first being God's creation of vegetation on the third day in Genesis 1:11 and His creation of plant life seemingly after He created humans in Genesis 2:5. This apparent contradiction may be explained by different Hebrew words for vegetation in each passage. Genesis 1:11 refers to plant life in general, while Genesis 2:5 refers to the vegetation Adam could care for and harvest for food.

Secondly, Genesis 1:24–25 says God created the animals early on the sixth creation day, while Genesis 2:19–20 seems to say that God created the animals *after* He created Adam. But these two passages can be reconciled by (accurately) viewing the second account as stating that God had *already* created the animals and then brought them to Adam "to see what he would call them. And whatever Adam called every living creature, that was its name. And Adam gave names to all cattle, and to the fowl of the air, and to every beast of the field" (Genesis 2:19–20).

MAIN ROAD

A Choice to Make (Genesis 2:15–17)

Adam and Eve had it made. They had the run of a beautiful garden, which their Creator visited every day. They could eat (almost) anything they wanted from the plant life that grew there. There was no sin or death—in fact, they had no concept of such things because no one had ever sinned or died. Adam and Eve could expect to live like this forever.

God had given the couple just one rule to follow: "Of every tree of the garden you may freely eat, but of the tree of the knowledge of good and evil, you shall not eat of it, for at the time when you eat of it, you shall surely die" (Genesis 2:16–17).

Tragically, Adam and Eve chose to disobey.

The Saddest Day in History (Genesis 3)

The first humans had nothing to fear because they lived in perfect harmony with God and with the animals that also inhabited the garden. But one day as Eve was by herself in the garden, she was approached by a talking serpent. The Bible's final book, Revelation, identifies the "old serpent" as the devil, or Satan.

Though the woman knew God had forbidden one tree's fruit on pain of death, the snake told her, "You shall not surely die, for God knows that in the day you eat from it, then your eyes shall be opened and you shall be as gods, knowing good and evil" (Genesis 3:4–5).

Eve was convinced. She picked a fruit and took a bite, then handed some to Adam. He too should have known better—but he took the fruit from Eve's hand and ate it.

What Is "Original Sin"?

After Adam and Eve disobeyed God, they suffered terrible consequences. But they were not the only ones—their children and their children's children, and all humans to this day, would be born into sin.

This is known as "original sin"—and it's the worst thing ever to happen to humanity. Sin affects everything about us, and it separates us from God. That's why Adam and Eve hid from Him after they disobeyed (Genesis 3:6).

Here are some verses that reference original sin and how it affects every one of us:

- ► "The LORD looked down from heaven on the children of men to see if there were any who understand and seek God. They have all turned aside; they have all together become filthy. There is no one who does good, no, not one" (Psalm 14:2–3).
- ► "Through one man sin entered into the world, and death through sin, and so death passed on to all men, for all have sinned" (Romans 5:12).
- ► "For as through one man's disobedience many were made sinners, so through the obedience of One many shall be made righteous" (Romans 5:19).
- ► "For since death came through man, the resurrection of the dead also came through man. For as in Adam all die, even so in Christ all shall be made alive" (1 Corinthians 15:21–22).

How Sin Changed Everything (Genesis 3:6–13)

At the moment Adam ate the forbidden fruit, things changed profoundly for him and his wife. For one thing, they both felt guilt for the first time. And they were embarrassed for having walked around the garden unclothed. They gathered fig leaves and made coverings to hide their naked bodies.

Worst of all, for the first time since God had made them, Adam and Eve were *afraid* of Him—so fearful that they hid themselves when they heard God in the garden. God asked the man where he was, not because He didn't know but so that Adam could admit to what he'd done. Adam answered, "I heard Your voice in the garden, and I was afraid because I was naked, and I hid myself" (Genesis 3:10).

Sin Brought Death (Genesis 3:14–24)

It was a terrible day for Adam and Eve, and for every human being who would live after them. Though God had said they would die if they ate from the tree of the knowledge of good and evil, they didn't immediately expire, at least physically. When Adam and Eve chose to sin, they died *spiritually*—in the sense that their relationship with the God who had created and loved them was ruined. They'd never again enjoy the pleasant relationship they'd been created to have with God. This is why the Bible says in the New Testament, "The wages of sin is death" (Romans 6:23).

God's Plan to Fix the Sin Problem

Though the whole world was now under a curse because of Adam and Eve's sin, God didn't leave humanity without hope. He had a plan to bring people back to Himself. That plan was to one day send a Messiah—a Savior—into the world to rescue us from sin. On the same day He banished Adam and Eve from the garden of Eden, He made the first of dozens of Old Testament prophecies regarding the Messiah:

> *And the* LORD *God said to the serpent, "Because you have done this, you are cursed above all cattle and above every beast of the field; on your belly you shall go, and you shall eat dust all the days of your life. And I will put enmity between you and the woman, and between your offspring and her offspring; He shall bruise your head, and you shall bruise His heel."*
> GENESIS 3:14–15

While the name *Jesus* and the word *Savior* don't appear in this passage, the idea is certainly there. Genesis 3:14–15 meant God would send a Savior who would be born from one of Eve's descendants—He would be born from a mother just like every other person.

Though Adam and Eve had failed in the worst possible way, and even though God punished them for what they had done, they were still His most prized creation. God would not simply cede them to the devil—nor all the people who would be born afterward.

God's Curses for Sin (Genesis 3:14–24)

Adam and Eve's sin had terrible consequences for them, for all who would follow them, and even for the physical world. God immediately cursed childbirth, which from then on would be a hard and painful experience for women, and He cursed the relationship between husbands and wives. God also placed a curse on the ground, meaning Adam, and every person to follow, would have to work hard to feed themselves. . . and then they would ultimately die. God banished Adam and Eve from the garden and placed a cherub (a type of angel) to guard the entrance so they couldn't return.

Sin Takes Hold of Humanity (Genesis 4, 6–10)

Genesis 4 reports how jealousy, anger, and even murder became a part of human life after Adam and Eve sinned—starting with their own children. In a fit of jealousy, Cain, the world's first child, killed his younger brother, because God had rejected Cain's sacrifice in favor of Abel's.

From this time forward, humans only became more and more evil. Things got so bad that God destroyed the whole world—and every living thing on it—in a massive flood. God instructed the world's only good man, Noah, to build a huge boat, called the ark. Noah and his family and two of every kind of animal would be saved from the flood, then repopulate the world after the water receded.

Did God Flood the Entire World, or Just the "Known World"?

Some people believe that God, in dealing with humanity's sin, flooded just the "known world." But the Bible clearly teaches that the entire earth was covered: "All the high hills that were under the whole heaven were covered" (Genesis 7:19), and "all flesh died that moved on the earth, both of fowl, and of cattle, and of beast, and of every creeping thing that creeps on the earth, and every man" (verse 21). Only Noah, his family, and the animals that boarded the ark with them remained alive.

In addition to the biblical record, there is much scientific evidence of a worldwide cataclysm such as a global flood. Every continent in the world contains vast fossil graveyards, and large numbers of coal and petroleum deposits throughout the world point to a rapid covering of vast quantities of vegetation.

3. GOD'S PEOPLE:
Israel as a Blessing to All Nations

MAIN ROAD

God Builds a Great Nation (Genesis 12–50)

In Genesis 3:14–15, God hinted at the Messiah He would send into the world to save human beings from their sin and its consequences. God didn't send Jesus into the world immediately, "but when the fullness of the time had come, God sent forth His Son, made of a woman, made under the law, to redeem those who were under the law, that we might receive the adoption of sons" (Galatians 4:4–5).

Starting in Genesis 12, the Bible shifts gears, telling how God began to establish the nation of Israel, through whom He would one day bring the Messiah into the world.

Israel's Founding Fathers (Genesis 12–50)

Israel's earliest days are defined by "patriarchal history." The word *patriarch* means "father," and those of Genesis are Abraham (Genesis 11:26–25:8), Isaac (21:1–35:28), and Jacob, whom God renamed "Israel" (25:21–50:14). When we call these men patriarchs, we're really calling them the fathers of the nation of Israel.

Jacob had twelve sons: Reuben, Simeon, Levi, Judah, Dan, Naphtali, Gad, Asher, Issachar, Zebulun, Joseph, and Benjamin. Each of his sons had families that grew into large groups of people called "tribes." These families came to be known as the "twelve tribes of Israel." Variously known as Israelites, Jews, or Hebrews, these twelve tribes would ultimately become a full-fledged nation with kings like Saul, David, and Solomon.

The Importance of the Nation of Israel

The nation of Israel plays a huge role in the Bible. . .and in God's plan to bring salvation to the world. Scripture shows that Israel was very special to God—the nation He Himself founded when He commanded Abraham to leave his longtime home and travel to a totally new place.

God first hinted at the Messiah just after Adam and Eve rebelled against Him (Genesis 3:14–15). By Genesis 12:1–3, God provided more detail: this Messiah would come from the line of Abraham, Isaac, and Jacob—Israel's patriarchs. For His own reasons, God chose a certain group of people as the origin of His promised Savior. Jesus would come through Israel.

Long before Jesus' birth, though, God wanted Israel to exemplify what serving Him really looks like. As a distinct people, Israel was to teach other nations about the Lord. Sadly, Israel usually failed in that assignment—but her people were still God's beloved.

Many centuries after the patriarchs, God said through the prophet Isaiah, "Yet now hear, O Jacob, My servant, and Israel, whom I have chosen. This is what the LORD says, who made you and formed you from the womb, who will help you: 'Do not fear, O Jacob, My servant, and you, Jeshurun, whom I have chosen'" (Isaiah 44:1–2). This and many other scriptures make it clear that among all the nations of the world, God chose *Israel* as His own special people.

God Calls Abraham (Genesis 12)

As the man God chose to be father of the nation of Israel, and as the spiritual father to Jews and Christians alike, Abraham (originally called Abram) is one of the most important people in scripture.

This is what the Bible says about God's initial call to Abram:

> Now the LORD had said to Abram, "Get out of your country, and from your family, and from your father's house, to a land that I will show you. And I will make of you a great nation, and I will bless you and make your name great, and you shall be a blessing. And I will bless those who bless you and curse him who curses you, and in you shall all families of the earth be blessed."
> GENESIS 12:1–3

God's Covenant Promise to Abram (Genesis 15)

Abram didn't question God, even to ask where he and his family would be going. He simply obeyed God, gathering his relatives and belongings and hitting the road. Abram left Haran, where he was living, and journeyed to Canaan, some six hundred miles away.

One night, many years later, God appeared to Abram and made an amazing promise. To an older man who had no children of his own, God said, "Look now toward heaven and count the stars, if you are able to number them. . . . So shall your descendants be" (Genesis 15:5). God was very pleased that Abram believed (Genesis 15:6).

God was about to do a great miracle in the lives of Abram and his wife, Sarai, later called Sarah.

Why Did God Choose Abram?

Genesis doesn't explain why God chose Abram to be the father of the Hebrew nation. But God had His own plans for the man He would rename Abraham, "for a father of many nations I have made you" (Genesis 17:5). The New Testament suggests that God chose Abraham because He knew him as a man of faith:

> *By faith Abraham obeyed when he was called to go out into a place that he would later receive as an inheritance. And he went out, not knowing where he went. By faith he sojourned in the land of promise as in a foreign country, dwelling in tents with Isaac and Jacob, the heirs with him of the same promise. For he looked for a city that has foundations, whose builder and maker is God.*
> HEBREWS 11:8–10

Like so many others whose stories are told in the Old Testament, Abraham was not a perfect man. But he believed God when He spoke, and this faith pleased God. That is why the Bible holds up Abraham as an example of what it takes to please God—namely, believing Him enough to obey His commands.

God's Promise of a Miracle Baby (Genesis 17)

God was ready to fulfill His promise to make Abraham the father of a great nation. That led to another promise, this one to give Abraham and his wife a son: "I will bless [Sarah] and give you a son from her also. Yes, I will bless her, and she shall be a mother of nations. Kings of people shall be from her" (Genesis 17:16).

At first, Abraham struggled to believe God's promise. The Bible says, "Abraham fell on his face and laughed and said in his heart, 'Shall a child be born to him who is a hundred years old? And shall Sarah, who is ninety years old, bear?'" (Genesis 17:17). But God told Abraham, "Sarah, your wife, shall bear you a son indeed, and you shall call his name Isaac, and I will establish My covenant with him for an everlasting covenant and with his descendants after him. . . . My covenant I will establish with Isaac, whom Sarah shall bear to you at this set time in the next year" (verses 19, 21).

God Delivers on His Promise (Genesis 18, 21)

When Sarah heard of God's promise to give her a son, she laughed inside. *I'm much too old to have a baby*, she thought. God knew of her laughing, though, and asked Abraham, "For what reason did Sarah laugh, saying, 'Shall I certainly bear a child, when I am old?' Is anything too hard for the LORD? At the time appointed I will return to you, according to the time of life, and Sarah shall have a son" (Genesis 18:13–14).

Indeed, God kept His promise of a miracle baby for Abraham and Sarah. "Who would have said to Abraham that Sarah should have nursed children?" she asked. "For I have borne him a son in his old age" (Genesis 21:7). God would use Isaac to continue His plan of establishing the nation of Israel and bringing salvation to the world.

Why Did God Tell Abraham to Kill Isaac?

One day, God told Abraham to do the unthinkable: "Take now your son, your only son Isaac, whom you love, and get into the land of Moriah, and offer him there for a burnt offering on one of the mountains of which I will tell you" (Genesis 22:2). What Abraham didn't know in that moment was that God was testing his faith.

Abraham obeyed, taking Isaac to Moriah, where he built an altar and prepared to sacrifice his son's life. But the Lord's angel stepped in at the last second, stopping Abraham from harming the boy. God said to Abraham, "Because you have done this thing and have not withheld your son, your only son, that in blessing I will bless you, and in multiplying I will multiply your descendants as the stars of the heaven, and as the sand that is on the seashore, and your descendants shall possess the gate of their enemies. And in your descendants shall all the nations of the earth be blessed, because you have obeyed My voice" (Genesis 22:16–18).

Abraham's willingness to sacrifice Isaac is an incredible example of obedience, even when God's commands don't make earthly sense. Abraham loved his son, and he knew that Isaac was a miraculous gift from God. But Abraham also trusted God to keep His promises. At the last possible minute, God came through for everyone.

God Continues the Family Line (Genesis 24–25)

Isaac was forty years old when he married a woman named Rebekah. But Rebekah, like Isaac's own mother, was unable to become pregnant—at least without God's help. Isaac prayed and asked God to give him and his wife a child, and God responded by blessing Rebekah with twins: Jacob and Esau. While Rebekah was pregnant, God told her, "Two nations are in your womb, and two kinds of people shall be separated from your body, and the one people shall be stronger than the other people, and the elder shall serve the younger" (Genesis 25:23). Though Jacob was born after Esau, he would eventually join the line of the patriarchs of Israel.

Jacob Steals His Brother's Birthright (Genesis 25:24–34)

Jacob literally means "deceiver," and he certainly lived up (or down) to his name. He was not always a great example for anyone to follow. Jacob had his strengths, but he also possessed some notable weaknesses—such as his dishonesty and willingness to do most anything to get what he wanted.

Because Esau had been born first, he was entitled to his father's wealth after Isaac died. But Jacob wanted the riches for himself, so one day he tricked his brother into selling his birthright. . .for a single bowl of soup. Later, Jacob and his mother, Rebekah, hatched a successful plan to trick Isaac into giving Jacob his fatherly blessing. As a result, Jacob—not Esau—became a forefather of the Jewish people (see Genesis 27).

How Could God Use a Man Like Jacob?

If you were to meet someone like Jacob, you'd do well not to get too close. Jacob was a cheat and a liar who did serious wrong to both his brother and father. But God didn't bless Jacob because he deserved goodness—God blessed Jacob because he was a part of the divine plan to establish the nation of Israel and bless the whole world.

At one point, with Esau pursuing him with thoughts of revenge, Jacob confessed to God, "I am not worthy of the least of all the mercies, and of all the truth, which You have shown to Your servant. . . . Deliver me, I ask You, from the hand of my brother, from the hand of Esau, for I fear him, lest he will come and strike me and the mothers with the children" (Genesis 32:10–11). Then he reminded God of His promises to his family, asking Him to keep His word.

God continued to work, making Jacob a patriarch to His chosen people. God also renamed him "Israel," which means "one who has struggled with God" (Genesis 32:22–31). Later, an entire nation—God's chosen nation—was named after him.

Jacob's Twelve Sons (Genesis 35, 37)

Jacob fathered twelve sons: Reuben, Simeon, Levi, Judah, Dan, Naphtali, Gad, Asher, Issachar, Zebulun, Joseph, and Benjamin. These men, apart from Levi, headed families that came to be known as the "twelve tribes of Israel." Joseph's family developed into two tribes, through his sons Ephraim and Manasseh.

The boys were born to two wives and two concubines. Not surprisingly, Jacob's family had problems. The Bible says that "Israel [Jacob] loved Joseph more than all his children, because he was the son of his old age, and he made him a coat of many colors. And when his brothers saw that their father loved him more than all his brothers, they hated him and could not speak peaceably to him" (Genesis 37:3–4).

The other sons knew their father favored Joseph, and they hated him for it. Joseph made matters worse by tattling to Jacob whenever his brothers did bad things. Finally, when Joseph told his brothers he had dreamed that they all bowed down to him (Genesis 37:5–11), they became angry enough to take action.

How God Brought Joseph to Egypt (Genesis 37:12–36)

Because Joseph's father favored him—and because Joseph antagonized his older brothers with his own words—the ten elder sons developed a hatred that bordered on murder. But the firstborn, Reuben, put a stop to his brothers' plan to kill Joseph by saying, "Do not shed blood, but cast him into this pit that is in the wilderness, and lay no hand on him" (Genesis 37:22). Reuben planned to return later and rescue Joseph. But while Reuben was away, the other brothers pulled Joseph out of the dry well and sold him to a group of Ishmaelite merchants passing by. They were carrying items to sell in Egypt, and they took Joseph with them. There, he became a slave.

Why Do Bad Things Happen to Good People?

Hated by his brothers, thrown into a dry well, and sold as a slave, Joseph found even more trouble in Egypt: he was imprisoned after his master's wife falsely accused him of attempted rape. In spite of his mistreatment, Joseph held to what was right in God's eyes.

By continuing to serve God through injustice, Joseph set an example for all believers to follow. God never promised His people a life without suffering or mistreatment. But He sometimes allows—even *causes*—suffering and unfair treatment when it helps to bring His perfect plans to reality.

That is why Joseph could ultimately tell his brothers, "You thought evil against me, but God meant it for good, to bring to pass, as it is this day, to save many people alive. Now therefore, do not fear. I will nourish you and your little ones" (Genesis 50:20–21).

Many centuries later, the apostle Paul wrote, "And we know that all things work together for good for those who love God, for those who are called according to His purpose" (Romans 8:28). It's possible that Paul was thinking of Joseph as he wrote those words.

Joseph's Life in Egypt (Genesis 39–41)

When Joseph arrived in Egypt, he was sold to a man named Potiphar, an important assistant to Pharaoh, king of Egypt. Potiphar was impressed with Joseph. He could see that Joseph was a trustworthy young man and that his God was with him. So Potiphar put Joseph in charge of his home and everything he owned. Unfortunately for Potiphar, his wife was attracted to Joseph—but he carefully avoided her advances. When she falsely accused Joseph of attempted rape, he was thrown in jail.

Some time later, God gave Joseph a break when Pharaoh had a strange dream that nobody could explain. Earlier, Joseph had interpreted dreams for two of Pharaoh's servants, who at the time were also prisoners. Joseph was summoned, interpreted Pharaoh's dream of a coming famine, and gave him advice for dealing with the disaster. Pharaoh was so impressed that he put Joseph in charge of the entire land of Egypt.

The Hebrews Travel to Egypt (Genesis 42–50)

Joseph continued to honor God, and he enjoyed great power, authority, and acclaim in Egypt. When the predicted famine arrived in the region, the Egyptians had more than enough grain stored away thanks to Joseph's wise counsel.

Meanwhile, back in Canaan (the "promised land," later to be known as Israel), the famine was causing fear and hunger. When Jacob heard that there was plenty of food in Egypt, he sent his sons to purchase what they could. They unknowingly appeared before Joseph, bowing to him just as the young man had dreamed many years before.

Ultimately, Joseph forgave his brothers and engineered a family reunion with Jacob, who thought for years that his beloved son was dead. The patriarch's extended family of seventy people soon moved to Egypt, where they enjoyed plenty of food and Joseph's protection.

The Book of Job

Many scholars believe Job lived around the time of the patriarchs. He was a righteous, godly man who suffered terribly. At the beginning of the book, Job was very wealthy, owning seven thousand sheep, three thousand camels, a thousand oxen, and five hundred female donkeys. He had a wife, seven sons, three daughters, and many servants (Job 1:2–3).

The story opens with a conversation in heaven between God and Satan. The devil told God that Job served Him faithfully only because of the blessings he'd receive. According to Satan, Job would curse God if he lost everything (Job 1:8–11). God knew that wasn't true, so He allowed the devil to test Job's faith and loyalty by afflicting him with terrible tragedies. Job lost all of his wealth, his ten children, and his own health.

The rest of the book covers Job's suffering and his response to it; his conversations with four "friends" who accused him of secret sin; and finally his conversation with God that put many things into perspective. In the end, Job knew his Lord even more deeply and was blessed with another family and twice his previous wealth.

Making a Home in Egypt (Exodus 1)

The Israelites stayed in Egypt, in a region called Goshen, for about 430 years after Jacob and his family arrived from Canaan. During that time, they built homes, married, and had children—lots of children. For many years, the Hebrews had it good in Egypt—but as their numbers grew, a new pharaoh grew worried. Fearing that the Israelites would become too powerful to control, or worse, might side with Egypt's enemies in a war, Pharaoh enslaved God's people. He made them build cities and roads for him, working them hard in hopes of preventing their further procreation.

God Sees His People's Afflictions
. . .and Acts (Exodus 2–3)

God saw the suffering of His people as they toiled under their Egyptian taskmasters. The Israelites were His chosen nation, and when the time was right, God tasked a man named Moses to lead the people out of their bondage.

Moses was an Israelite born during their slavery in Egypt. He miraculously escaped Pharaoh's decree to drown male Hebrew babies in the Nile, and even more miraculously was adopted by Pharaoh's daughter. Growing up in the Egyptian palace, he still recognized his Israelite heritage, and one day he killed an Egyptian taskmaster who was abusing a Hebrew. Moses then fled to Midian.

There, while Moses was working as a shepherd for a man named Jethro, God spoke to Moses from a burning bush. "I have surely seen the affliction of My people who are in Egypt and have heard their cry because of their taskmasters, for I know their sorrows," God told him. "Come now, therefore, and I will send you to Pharaoh, that you may bring forth My people, the children of Israel, out of Egypt" (Exodus 3:7, 10).

What Makes Moses So Important?

Moses is known as the great deliverer who freed his fellow Israelites from their Egyptian slavery. He stood up to Pharaoh, then the most powerful man in the world, demanding that he set the Hebrews free. When Pharaoh simply mocked, Moses didn't lose heart. He stood aside and let the Lord do what Moses couldn't do himself—namely, convince Pharaoh that it was in his best interest to let the Israelites go.

Though he wasn't the most confident leader—at least at first—Moses chose to obey and trust God. He led the people out of Egypt, through the miraculously separated Red Sea, then for years of wilderness wandering to the edge of the "promised land" of Canaan. Moses received the laws God wanted His people to follow (the Ten Commandments, as well as many others) and also found time to write the first five books of the Bible—Genesis, Exodus, Leviticus, Numbers, and Deuteronomy, collectively known as the "Pentateuch."

Most impressively, Moses was identified as a friend of God (Exodus 33:11).

A Reluctant Deliverer (Exodus 4)

Moses is a hero to both Jews and Christians because of his leadership of God's people. But when Moses first heard God's call from the burning bush, he didn't believe he was the right man for the job. Moses questioned his own qualifications and complained that he wasn't a great speaker. His excuses angered God, but the Lord still promised to be with Moses as he went to Egypt to confront Pharaoh. God also gave Moses miraculous powers to use while facing the Egyptian ruler. Finally, God commissioned Moses' brother, Aaron, as the official mouthpiece of the mission: "I know that he can speak well," God said. "You shall speak to him and put words in his mouth" (Exodus 4:14–15).

Moses Confronts Pharaoh (Exodus 5)

With Aaron in tow, Moses met with Pharaoh and demanded, in the name of God, that all the Israelites be allowed to leave Egypt. Pharaoh refused, though, several times, telling Moses and Aaron, "Who is the LORD, that I should obey His voice to let Israel go? I do not know the LORD; neither will I let Israel go" (Exodus 5:2).

But Pharaoh didn't get the last word. To break his stubbornness, God sent ten terrible plagues on Egypt—the Nile River turning to blood (Exodus 7:17–18), frogs (8:1–4), lice (8:16–17), flies (8:20–22), the death of livestock (9:1–4), sores on people and animals (9:8–9), hail (9:22–23), locusts (10:4–5), darkness (10:21–22), and the death of all firstborn (11:4–7).

Passover

Passover, the celebration of the Israelites' departure (or "exodus") from Egypt, is still an important Jewish holiday. As the last of the plagues, God announced He was going to wipe out all the firstborn of humans and livestock in Egypt. The Israelites could avoid this tragedy by smearing lamb's blood over the doors of their homes. God would "pass over" every home that had the blood. After this plague, Pharaoh finally ordered the Israelites to leave Egypt (Exodus 12:31–32).

Blood is an important subject in the Bible. Leviticus 17:11–14 indicates that the life of living creatures is in the blood. When people in Old Testament times sinned, they had to shed the blood of a flawless animal as a "sacrifice." This meant that the person did not have to die for his own sin—it was covered, temporarily, by the sacrifice. The New Testament book of Hebrews says, "By the law almost all things are purified with blood, and without the shedding of blood there is no remission [payment of sin]" (9:22). Jesus, whose life, death, and resurrection introduced the "New Testament," became the flawless, once-for-all sacrifice for all humanity. When the blood of the perfect "Passover Lamb" was shed, all other sacrifices became obsolete. Now, faith in Jesus' work removes our sin.

The Israelites Leave Egypt (Exodus 12)

After the death of every firstborn in Egypt, including his own son, Pharaoh finally freed the Israelites. He sent for Moses and Aaron that night and told them, "Rise up, and get out from among my people, both you and the children of Israel. And go serve the LORD as you have said. Also take your flocks and your herds, as you have said, and be gone. And bless me also" (Exodus 12:31–32). The people of Egypt were afraid they would all die if the Israelites stayed, so they urged them on with gifts of clothing, gold, and jewels. The people of Israel—about six hundred thousand men plus many more women and children—left Egypt having "spoiled the Egyptians" (Exodus 12:36).

Pharaoh's Last Shot (Exodus 14)

The Bible says that after the Hebrews left Egypt, "the LORD hardened the heart of Pharaoh, king of Egypt, and he pursued after the children of Israel" (Exodus 14:8). Pharaoh's army chased the Israelites, who were terrified when they saw horses and chariots coming. But God led the people through the Red Sea, which He miraculously parted for them. Then He caused the waters to rush back into place, drowning Pharaoh's army as it tried to follow.

The Hebrews were now completely free to journey to the promised land. As it turned out, this relatively short trip would take forty years to complete. Along the way, the Israelites would suffer much of God's discipline, see many of His miracles, and receive His entire law, the rules and regulations that would govern their lives in Canaan.

The Promised Land

God freed the Israelites from their Egyptian slavery so they could make the journey to the promised land. This land—also called Canaan—is what God promised to Abraham and his descendants in Genesis 12:7. God later repeated this promise to Abraham's son Isaac (Genesis 26:3) and then to Isaac's son Jacob (Genesis 28:13). The promised land was a gift from the Creator to His chosen people, the place where they would establish their nation. God guided the people of Israel to their promised land by His own presence and through His miraculous works (Exodus 33:14–16).

Canaan was named after a grandson of Noah. It lay mostly between the Mediterranean Sea and the Jordan River. Today, Israel, the West Bank, the Gaza Strip, and parts of Lebanon and Syria share this land.

God Gives Moses the Ten Commandments (Exodus 19–20)

The Israelites had seen God perform stunning miracles to break them out of Egypt. The miraculous provision of food and water highlighted the early months of their journey to Canaan. Three months after they had left Egypt, the Israelites camped in the wilderness at the foot of Mount Sinai. Moses scaled the mountain, far from the people, where he spent forty days alone with God. There, God gave Moses the Ten Commandments and other laws that would help the people live blessed lives. God inscribed the Ten Commandments on two stone tablets, which Moses would carry back down the mountain.

The Purpose of the Ten Commandments (Exodus 20:1–17)

The Ten Commandments are laws that summarize the hundreds of specific rules given to Moses. God gave His law to the Israelites to guide them in their new lives in the promised land. The first of God's Ten Commandments is "You shall have no other gods before Me" (Exodus 20:3). God had chosen the people of Israel as His own, brought them out of slavery in Egypt, and established them as a nation. He had no intention of sharing their affection with idols and false gods.

The Ten Commandments

▶ You shall have no other gods before Me.

▶ You shall not make for yourself any graven image, or any likeness of anything that is in heaven above, or that is in the earth beneath, or that is in the water under the earth.

▶ You shall not take the name of the LORD your God in vain, for the LORD will not hold him guiltless who takes His name in vain.

▶ Remember the Sabbath day, to keep it holy. Six days you shall labor and do all your work, but the seventh day is the Sabbath of the LORD your God.

▶ Honor your father and your mother, that your days may be long on the land that the LORD your God gives you.

▶ You shall not kill.

▶ You shall not commit adultery.

▶ You shall not steal.

▶ You shall not bear false witness against your neighbor.

▶ You shall not covet your neighbor's house. You shall not covet your neighbor's wife, or his manservant, or his maidservant, or his ox, or his donkey, or anything that is your neighbor's.

God Gives the Israelites the Law (Leviticus)

Having delivered the Israelites out of Egypt, God spoke through Moses, instructing the people in how to live, how to treat one another, and how to worship. These laws are found in the book of Leviticus, which includes a system of sacrifices that would one day be replaced by the ultimate sacrifice of Jesus Christ on the cross. According to ancient Jewish tradition, the law of Moses contains 613 different commandments, each of which fits into one of three categories: civil, ceremonial, or moral.

Types of Laws (Leviticus)

Civil laws were the rules of daily living. They covered everything from murder to the repayment for wrongs done by one person to another. Civil laws also dealt with kindness for the poor (Leviticus 19:9–10), debt (Leviticus 25:35–46), theft (Leviticus 19:11), and many other topics.

Ceremonial laws involved Israel's worship of God. They included festivals (Leviticus 23), dietary laws (Leviticus 11), priestly duties (Leviticus 8–9), and various sin offerings (Leviticus 1–7).

Finally, moral laws concerned personal living and reflected God's holy nature. They include laws concerning idolatry (Leviticus 19:4), honoring of parents (Leviticus 19:3), and various sexual sins (Leviticus 18:20, 20:10–21). These laws are still in effect for Christians today.

Why Do Christians Follow Some Laws of Leviticus but Not Others?

God expects Christians today to follow His moral laws, which are all affirmed in the New Testament. The civil laws were specific to the ancient nation of Israel. The ceremonial laws were all fulfilled when Jesus died a sacrificial death on the cross. His own teaching and the rest of the New Testament tell us very clearly that God does not require Christians to follow Old Testament laws on diet, animal sacrifices, feasts, ritual cleanliness, and so on (see Romans 2:25–29, Galatians 2:15–16, and Ephesians 2:15, for example).

Christians today can find guidance on God's character and ways from the Old Testament laws. But the New Testament is the guide as to which rules apply now. The New Testament, which came into effect with the life, death, and resurrection of Jesus, is God's most current communication with His people.

God Leads His People toward the Promised Land (Numbers)

The book of Numbers tells of the Israelites' journey from Mount Sinai, where they received the law, to the border of the promised land. They had been freed from slavery in Egypt and brought to the very border of Canaan, where they could take possession of a beautiful land God had already given them. But the people's ingratitude, unbelief, and disobedience led to a punishment of *forty years* of wandering in the wilderness—four decades they should have spent in their land of promise.

God Delays the Israelites' Entry into the Promised Land (Numbers 13–14)

Moses sent twelve spies—one from each tribe—to scout out the promised land. Ten of the spies returned with frightening reports of giants in the land. It would be foolish, they warned, for the Israelites to try to take the land. The other two spies, Joshua and Caleb, believed the Israelites could easily take the land, since God was with them. Sadly, the Israelites listened to the negative report.

God said to Moses, "How long will these people provoke Me? And how long will it be before they believe Me, for all the signs that I have showed among them?" (Numbers 14:11). God was ready to destroy the Israelites and make a new nation from Moses' line. But Moses prayed for the people and God spared them. However, He declared that Israel would not enter the promised land for another forty years. Only Joshua and Caleb of the current leadership generation would see Canaan—all of the others would die in the wilderness.

The "Good Spies" of Israel

When twelve spies were sent ahead to investigate the promised land, a large majority of them—ten—reported that trying to conquer Canaan was a fool's errand. There were giants in the land, they said, too big and powerful for the Israelites to overcome. Only two spies, Joshua and Caleb, gave a positive report. They said the Israelites could easily defeat the inhabitants of the land.

Joshua is first mentioned in the Bible in Exodus 17:9, where Moses commands him to choose and lead men in battle against the Amalekites, a people group that lived south of Canaan. Later, Joshua would heroically lead the Israelites into their promised land. For his part, Caleb requested a section of the promised land at age eighty-five, promising to drive out any giants he found there (Joshua 14:6–15).

Joshua and Caleb were faithful men who believed God's promises and acted on them. They recognized the strength of the giants of Canaan, but they knew their God was far more powerful.

Moses Disqualifies Himself from the Promised Land (Numbers 20:7–12)

Moses had led the people of Israel brilliantly, but he was banished from the promised land for disobeying God. When the people complained that they were thirsty, God told Moses to speak to a large rock, which would then miraculously produce water. But Moses, angry with the people's grumbling, struck the rock twice with his shepherd's staff. God still provided the water, but He told Moses, "Because you did not believe Me, to sanctify Me in the eyes of the children of Israel, therefore you shall not bring this congregation into the land that I have given them" (Numbers 20:12).

The Miracle of the Bronze Serpent (Numbers 21:5–9)

The bronze serpent was a metal image that God used to heal people from snakebites. Many of the Israelites complained against both Moses and God for leading them into the wilderness. In response, God sent venomous snakes into the camp. As people suffered and died, Moses prayed for them, and God instructed him to craft a snake from bronze. Anyone who had been bitten by a real snake could look at the bronze serpent and be healed.

Centuries later, Jesus likened Himself to that bronze serpent, saying, "As Moses lifted up the serpent in the wilderness, even so the Son of Man must be lifted up, that whoever believes in Him should not perish but have eternal life" (John 3:14–15).

The Sad, Strange Story of Balaam

Balaam was a mysterious prophet who sometimes heard from God but does not seem to have been part of God's people (Numbers 22–24). He is remembered as the man whose donkey had to talk sense into him.

The king of Moab, Balak, wanted Balaam to curse Israel. Balak was going to pay for Balaam's cursing, but God warned Balaam to speak only the Lord's words.

The next morning, Balaam saddled his donkey and headed out to meet Balak. But God stopped Balaam by sending an angel to block the donkey's path. Balaam beat the poor animal three times, before God gave it the ability to talk (Numbers 22:28). Soon, Balaam also saw the angel, which was prepared to kill him. The donkey had saved Balaam's life!

In Moab, Balak three times ordered Balaam to speak a curse on Israel, but each time Balaam spoke a blessing instead. The king was infuriated and sent the prophet away without pay.

The "Second Law" (Deuteronomy)

In Deuteronomy, the fifth and final book of the Pentateuch, Moses spoke to the generation of Israelites born after God delivered their elders out of Egypt. Many of the younger Israelites had undoubtedly heard about what God had done for their parents in the previous forty years. But now that they were about to enter the promised land, Moses wanted to remind them of God's law—*Deuteronomy* means "second law." Moses spoke to the people four times, reminding them where they had come from, where they had been, whom they belonged to, and how they should live. Much of the book contains Moses' recitation of Israel's history, and a reminder of God's expectations for the nation.

Moses' Death (Deuteronomy 34)

Moses had provided excellent leadership to Israel during the last forty years of his life. Sadly, though, one moment of disobedience cost him the honor of leading the people into the promised land. The final chapter of Deuteronomy says Moses climbed to the top of Mount Nebo, where God showed him the promised land of Canaan and said to him, "This is the land that I swore to Abraham, to Isaac, and to Jacob, saying, 'I will give it to your descendants.' I have caused you to see it with your eyes, but you shall not go over there" (Deuteronomy 34:4). Moses died in Moab at the age of 120. Then God "buried him in a valley in the land of Moab, across from Beth-peor, but no man knows of his burial place to this day" (verse 6).

SIDE ROAD

Joshua

Shortly before Moses' death, God said to him, "Behold, your days approach when you must die. Call Joshua, and present yourselves in the tabernacle of the congregation, that I may give him a charge" (Deuteronomy 31:14). Moses and Joshua did as God commanded, and the torch of leadership was passed.

Joshua is first mentioned in Exodus 17:9, where Moses commands him to lead soldiers into battle against Amalek. (This is the battle that prospered as long as Moses raised his arms over the action; when he tired, Aaron and Hur helped him to keep his hands up high.) Later, Moses made Joshua one of the twelve spies tasked with scouting out the promised land (Numbers 13).

Deuteronomy 34:9 says that "Joshua the son of Nun was full of the spirit of wisdom, for Moses had laid his hands on him. And the children of Israel listened to him and did as the LORD commanded Moses."

New Leader, Same Mission (Joshua 1)

After the death of Moses, Joshua assumed the mantle of leadership. Under his wise and strong direction, the Israelites captured and settled their promised land. God had given Joshua a task impossible to accomplish in his own strength. But when God said, "Be strong and of good courage. Do not be afraid or be dismayed, for the LORD your God is with you wherever you go" (Joshua 1:9), Joshua believed and obeyed. As a result, God made Joshua a great leader in the eyes of all his people (Joshua 4:14).

Israel's Miraculous Entry into Canaan (Joshua 3–4)

To enter the promised land, the Israelites had to cross the Jordan River. River crossings are always a challenge, but at this time the river was running so high it had overflowed its banks. God, however, can always make a way. As soon as the feet of the priests, who were carrying the ark of the covenant, touched the water, the river stopped flowing far upstream. That allowed the Israelites to cross, while the priests stood in the middle of the dry riverbed (Joshua 3:15–17). After hundreds of years of waiting —including the past forty years of wandering in the wilderness—the Israelites were now in the land God had promised them.

The Memorial of the Twelve Stones

After all the Israelites had crossed the Jordan River, God commanded Joshua, "Take twelve men out from the people, one man from every tribe, and command them, saying, 'Take for yourselves twelve stones from here out of the middle of the Jordan, out of the place where the priests' feet stood firm, and you shall carry them over with you and leave them in the lodging place where you shall lodge this night'" (Joshua 4:2–3).

Joshua told the stone carriers, "When your children ask their fathers in the future, saying, 'What do you mean by these stones?' Then you shall answer them that the waters of the Jordan were cut off before the ark of the covenant of the LORD. When it crossed over the Jordan, the waters of the Jordan were cut off. And these stones shall be a memorial to the children of Israel forever" (Joshua 4:6–7).

The men placed the stones in the middle of the riverbed, where the priests had stood. The Bible says, "They are there to this day" (Joshua 4:9). . .the day that the book of Joshua was written.

The Israelites' Work in Canaan (Joshua 6–21)

The book of Joshua recounts Israel's taking of the promised land of Canaan. Chapter 6 describes the conquest of the seemingly impenetrable city of Jericho. After a setback due to the disobedience of a man named Achan (chapter 7), the Israelites conquered the city of Ai. With Joshua leading the charge, the Israelites subdued all of southern Canaan (chapters 9–10), then defeated a coalition of northern Canaanite kings (chapter 11).

Though the people of Israel had traveled as a group since leaving Egypt, they were still a collection of twelve tribes. Joshua's final task in life was to assign each tribe its own section of the promised land. That story is told in Joshua 13–21.

Joshua's Farewell (Joshua 24)

Shortly before Joshua died, he reminded the people of the miraculous things God had done for them. And he encouraged the people to remain faithful to Him: "Now therefore, fear the LORD, and serve Him in sincerity and in truth, and put away the gods that your fathers served on the other side of the flood and in Egypt, and serve the LORD. And if it seems evil to you to serve the LORD, choose for yourselves this day whom you will serve, whether the gods that your fathers served who were on the other side of the flood, or the gods of the Amorites, in whose land you dwell. But as for me and my house, we will serve the LORD" (Joshua 24:14–15).

Joshua died at the age of 110. He was buried in a place called Timnath-serah.

The "Battle of Jericho"

Jericho was surrounded by high, thick walls that protected the city from even the most formidable invaders. But God gave Joshua an unusual battle plan for taking the city (Joshua 6:1–5). Joshua should command his soldiers to march around the city once a day for six days. On the seventh day, the soldiers would march around the city seven times as the priests blew their horns. When the priests gave one long blast, all the people would shout. And the city walls would fall before them!

The "battle of Jericho" really wasn't much of a battle. The Israelites followed God's plan and "when the people heard the sound of the trumpet and the people shouted with a great shout. . .the wall fell down flat, so that the people went up into the city, every man straight before him, and they took the city" (Joshua 6:20).

Special Deliverers (Judges)

The book of Judges describes leaders who bravely stepped up when the people of Israel—due to their own disobedience—were oppressed by foreign powers. These thirteen people are called *judges*, a term indicating "deliverers." The period of the judges lasted around 350 years, starting sometime after 1400 BC. The judges include Othniel, Ehud, Shamgar, Deborah, Gideon, Abimelech, Tola, Jair, Jephthah, Ibzan, Elon, Abdon, and Samson.

In the judges' day, Israel had no king—and most people didn't want one. God was their King, though they often strayed from Him. So He raised up the judges to take responsibility for the nation. The book of Judges describes a dreary cycle: The people would follow God for a while, then fall away. God would allow other nations to dominate the Israelites until they cried out to Him. Then He would send a judge to deliver them from their enemies.

Othniel: Israel's First Judge (Judges 3:9–11)

Judges 3:7–8 says that "the children of Israel did evil in the sight of the Lord, and they forgot the Lord their God and served the Baals and the Asherim [false gods]. Therefore the anger of the Lord burned against Israel, and He sold them into the hand of Chushan-rishathaim, king of Mesopotamia." After serving under his oppressive rule for eight years, the people of Israel cried out to God, who sent Othniel, Israel's first recorded judge. He successfully led the people in a war against Mesopotamia, and the Israelites then lived in peace for forty years.

How Could God Use a Man Like Samson?

Samson, the last of the judges in this book of the Bible (Judges 13–16), showed amazing courage and strength on behalf of the people of Israel. The Bible says Samson once killed thirty enemy Philistines single-handedly (Judges 14:19). He also killed a thousand Philistines with the jawbone of a donkey (15:12–15), and he wiped out many more by pushing down the pillars that held up the Philistine temple (16:26–30). Samson was able to do such things when "the Spirit of the LORD came mightily on him" (Judges 14:6).

Yet Samson wasn't the kind of man most of us would see as a servant of God. He was selfish and prideful, always trying to get his own way. He never seemed to consider the consequences of his actions, sometimes pursuing an unholy desire for women—even Philistine women, one of whom conspired with Israel's enemy to kill him. But Samson was still God's choice to judge Israel. Judges 2:18 says, "When the LORD raised up judges for them, then the LORD was with the judge"—even one as flawed as Samson.

Judge Deborah (Judges 4:4–5:31)

Deborah was the fourth of the judges—and the only woman in the group. She became judge after Jabin, the king of Canaan, had ruled over Israel for twenty years. As a prophetess, Deborah was a wise and respected woman who faithfully spoke the words God gave her. They included God's instructions to a man named Barak to gather an army and fight the Canaanites. But when Barak balked, Deborah joined him in battle. Because of her heroic leadership in the face of great adversity, she is considered one of the most important women of the Bible.

Gideon, Israel's Greatest Judge (Judges 6:1–8:32)

God used Gideon to free Israel from oppression by the Midianites—and that led to peace in Israel for forty years. With arguably Israel's greatest judge in the lead, three hundred Israelite warriors defeated a massive Midianite army, "as numerous as grasshoppers" (Judges 7:12), and drove them away. The victory was God's work through Gideon, and he wisely resisted the people's call for him to become king. "I will not rule over you, nor shall my son rule over you," Gideon said. "The LORD shall rule over you" (Judges 8:23). Gideon lived to old age and was buried in his father's grave. Sadly, the people forgot everything God had done for them through Gideon. They turned away from the one true God and worshipped a false god called Baal-berith.

Who Was Ruth. . .and Why Does She Matter?

Ruth was a young woman from Moab, a neighbor and some-time enemy of Israel. She married into an Israelite family that had moved to Moab to escape a famine in Judah; when Ruth's husband and father-in-law both died in quick succession, she pledged faithfulness to her mother-in-law, Naomi, moving with her to Bethlehem after the famine ended. There, Ruth met and married a wealthy farmer named Boaz.

Ruth plays an important role in the bigger story of God's plan to bring salvation into the world. Though she was not an Israelite, her marriage to Boaz produced a son named Obed, who had a son named Jesse, who had a son named David—who became Israel's greatest king. Because Jesus Christ descended from David, Ruth was an ancestor of the Savior. In Matthew 1, she is one of five women mentioned in Jesus' genealogy.

Prophets and Kings (1 Samuel)

The book of 1 Samuel tells two major stories. The first is the account of the beloved prophet Samuel, Israel's last judge (chapters 1–12). The rest of the book describes the establishment of a monarchy (a government led by a king) in Israel. When the people cried out for a king, God gave them what they wanted. He identified Saul and had Samuel anoint him, but his reign ultimately failed. God then chose a young shepherd named David to be Israel's second king.

How Saul Became King (1 Samuel 8–10)

The prophet Samuel had two sons—Joel and Abijah—and he appointed both to be judges. But Joel and Abijah were ungodly men who used their important position for selfish gain. The elders of Israel told Samuel that he was becoming too old to lead and that they did not trust his sons to follow him. They demanded a king to rule over Israel (1 Samuel 8:1–5).

God recognized that this demand was a rejection of His own leadership, but He granted Israel the king they craved. God selected Saul, the handsome son of a wealthy man named Kish, to lead Israel. Saul started his reign well, around 1050 BC, uniting the people to defeat their enemies, including the dreaded Philistines.

But pride led Saul to make some terrible decisions. After forty years, God removed him from the throne.

The Philistines

As you read the Old Testament, you'll often see the Philistines mentioned. They were a warlike people who lived southwest of Israel, between the Mediterranean Sea and the Jordan River. Worshippers of false gods, the Philistines were Israel's archenemy for several centuries. Leaders like Samson, Samuel, Saul, and David all had to deal with the Philistines' aggression. The most famous was the giant warrior Goliath, whom David—just a shepherd boy at the time—killed with a stone shot from his sling.

Early in Israel's history, God had promised to give the Philistines' land to His people (Exodus 23:31). But when the Israelites failed to destroy all the inhabitants of Canaan, God allowed some—like the Philistines—to "test Israel" (Judges 3:4). By the time of the judges and kings of Israel, the Philistines were a powerful enemy of God's people. They even once captured the ark of the covenant, though that didn't turn out well for them (see 1 Samuel 4–5).

David Chosen as Israel's Second King (1 Samuel 16)

God ultimately rejected Israel's first king. Saul's successor would be revealed by the prophet Samuel. God sent Samuel to Bethlehem, to meet the sons of a man named Jesse. Samuel reviewed the seven oldest sons, thinking at one point, "Surely the LORD's anointed is before Him" (1 Samuel 16:6). But God rejected each of them, saying, "Do not look at his appearance or at the height of his stature, because I have refused him. . . . Man looks at the outward appearance, but the LORD looks at the heart" (verse 7). Finally, Samuel was introduced to Jesse's youngest son, the shepherd boy David. God said to Samuel, "Arise, anoint him, for this is he" (verse 12). Samuel poured oil over David's head, and "the Spirit of the LORD came on David from that day forward" (verse 13).

David's Rise, Saul's Decline (1 Samuel 17–31)

Over time, David's popularity with the people of Israel grew—due in part to his victory over the Philistine giant, Goliath. Saul, who was still king when David was anointed, recognized that the people loved David. He also knew that God had chosen David to replace him. In a jealous rage, Saul wanted to kill the young man and made multiple attempts on David's life. But David never tried to fight back; instead, he ran, trying to stay out of Saul's reach until it was his own time to be king. Even when he had a chance to kill Saul, David refused. He considered Saul as God's anointed king until it was clearly God's time for David to be crowned (1 Samuel 26:10–11).

How Could a Shepherd Boy Defeat a Battle-Hardened Giant?

Israel was facing the Philistines in war. One of those Philistines was Goliath, who was otherworldly large. The Bible says he stood some nine feet tall. His armor and weapons were all as supersized as he was. Israel's soldiers were terrified of Goliath.

Then in stepped a shepherd boy, offering to take battle to the giant. The young man told King Saul, "Let no man's heart fail because of him; your servant will go and fight with this Philistine" (1 Samuel 17:32). Saul tried to discourage David, but Jesse's youngest son insisted that he had already killed a bear and a lion, though not in his own strength. "The LORD who delivered me out of the paw of the lion and out of the paw of the bear, He will deliver me out of the hand of this Philistine" (verse 37).

Goliath wasn't impressed with David's size. But the shepherd boy announced that he was fighting in the name of the Lord and that God would help him kill Goliath (1 Samuel 17:45–46). David then loaded his sling with one of the small rocks he'd taken from a stream. He slung the rock, hitting Goliath square in the forehead, toppling him to the ground. Then David took Goliath's own sword and cut off the giant's head!

David Becomes King (2 Samuel)

The book of 2 Samuel begins where 1 Samuel ends. Saul is dead, having taken his own life after being wounded in battle with the Philistines. David is first crowned in Judah, the southern section of Israel encompassing Jerusalem, where he will rule for seven years. Then he became ruler of all Israel, reigning for an additional thirty-three years over the united kingdom. The author of 2 Samuel gives readers an honest look at David—both the great things he did and his terrible decisions, including his sin with Bathsheba.

David's Achievements as King (2 Samuel, 1 Chronicles 11–29)

David accomplished much for God and for the kingdom of Israel during his reign as king. He unified the twelve tribes into one great and powerful nation and made Jerusalem its capital city. He is considered Israel's greatest king, whose military victories ushered in a period of peace in which his son Solomon built God's temple, Israel's first permanent worship center. David also wrote at least seventy-three of the psalms we find in the Bible. Most important of all, David was known as "a man after God's own heart," who—despite his obvious flaws—loved and served the Lord, becoming an ancestor of the Messiah, Jesus Christ.

The "Davidic Covenant"

This is a series of promises God made to David through the prophet Nathan in 2 Samuel 7 and later summarized in 1 Chronicles 17:11–14 and 2 Chronicles 6:16. In the Davidic Covenant, God promised David that the Messiah would come from his lineage. God would establish an eternal kingdom for this descendant of David. The promise was unconditional, meaning its fulfillment did not depend on David's (or Israel's) obedience but solely on God's faithfulness to His own word.

The Davidic Covenant starts with God's reaffirmation of the promise of land that He had made to Abraham (2 Samuel 7:10). God also promised that David's son (Solomon) would succeed him as king of Israel and build a temple as a place of worship (verses 12–13).

The promise continued, expansively: "I will establish the throne of his kingdom forever" (2 Samuel 7:13), and "Your house and your kingdom shall be established forever before you. Your throne shall be established forever" (verse 16). This part of the covenant referred to the future Messiah, who would be born to David's line, and who would rule forever. Though this was mysterious to David, we know the promise refers to Jesus.

David's Sin (2 Samuel 11)

David was a great leader but far from perfect. He had multiple wives and did not always properly discipline his children. And one time, when he spied the beautiful wife of one of his loyal warriors bathing, he had the woman brought to him. After David's adultery with Bathsheba, she informed him that she was pregnant. David tried to hide his sin by arranging to have her husband, Uriah, killed in battle. David then married her, but his actions "displeased the LORD" (2 Samuel 11:27). The prophet Nathan confronted David over his egregious sin, and the king acknowledged his wrongdoing. God forgave David, but there would be serious ongoing consequences of his failure.

How David's Sin Affected Him and His Kingdom (2 Samuel 12)

When David confessed, Nathan assured him that God had forgiven him—he wasn't going to die. But Nathan also announced the consequences of David's folly. First, the baby he'd conceived with Bathsheba would die. Not only that, but David's family would be plagued by violence. This prophecy was fulfilled when one of David's sons, Absalom, killed a half brother, Amnon, who had violated Absalom's sister. Absalom then carried out a plot to remove David from power and take his crown. His army nearly defeated David's forces, but God intervened on David's behalf. Joab, David's military commander, killed Absalom against David's wishes.

How Could David Be "A Man after God's Own Heart"?

Israel's first king, Saul, did some good things but ultimately made terrible decisions that led to his downfall. Initially, he offered a sacrifice without God's approval (1 Samuel 13:9–14). Then he spared the Amalekites' king and best livestock, disobeying God's order to destroy them all (1 Samuel 15:3). Finally, he lied to Samuel, God's prophet, about what he had done.

That's when God decided to replace Saul. "The LORD has sought for Himself a man after His own heart," Samuel declared, "and the LORD has commanded him to be captain over His people because you have not kept what the LORD commanded you" (1 Samuel 13:14).

As it turns out, David would also make a number of poor decisions as Israel's king. Some of them had disastrous consequences for him, his family, and his nation. But in spite of his many weaknesses, David truly loved God. When he failed, he acknowledged his guilt, confessed his sin, and always returned to the Lord.

Solomon Becomes Israel's Third King (1 Kings 1:1–2:11)

Though the baby conceived in David's adultery with Bathsheba died shortly after birth, the now-married couple soon had a second child. David named him Solomon. Years later, when David was on his death-bed, another son—Adonijah—prepared to take the throne as Israel's third king. But Bathsheba and the prophet Nathan went to David to remind him of his promise that Solomon would succeed him. God had told David that Solomon was His choice for king (1 Chronicles 22:6–10). After Solomon was anointed, David reminded him of what would make him successful: "Keep the charge of the LORD your God, to walk in His ways, to keep His statutes and His commandments and His judgments and His testimonies, as it is written in the law of Moses" (1 Kings 2:3).

Solomon's Wise Request of God (1 Kings 3:6–15)

Solomon had huge shoes to fill. He wanted to be a great king like his father but wasn't sure he was able. After becoming king of Israel, while visiting a place called Gibeon, Solomon saw God in a dream. The Lord said, "Ask. What shall I give you?" (1 Kings 3:5). Solomon quickly replied, "Give Your servant an understanding heart to judge Your people, that I may discern between good and bad. For who is able to judge this great people of Yours?" (verse 9). God was very pleased with that request, so He gave Solomon "a wise and understanding heart" (verse 12) in addition to great riches and honor.

How Wise Was Solomon?

Early in his kingship, Solomon's wisdom was tested by an argument between two prostitutes. They lived together and had each had a baby boy around the same time. One night, one of the women rolled over on her baby, killing him. When she took the other woman's child as her own, she started a dispute that ended up before the king.

Solomon listened to their bickering for a while, then called for a sword. "Divide the living child in two," he commanded, "and give half to the one and half to the other" (1 Kings 3:25). Immediately, one woman cried out, "O my lord, give her the living child and in no way slay him" (verse 26). This response told Solomon exactly who the mother was. All of Israel heard about the ruling "and they feared the king" (verse 28).

He is credited with speaking three thousand proverbs (1 Kings 4:32), many of which are included in the book of Proverbs. Solomon is also the likely author of the book of Ecclesiastes, which shows how meaningless life is—even a life of wealth and ease—when God is not a person's priority.

Solomon's Temple (1 Kings 5–6)

When he became king, Solomon dedicated himself to faithfully serving God, and that meant the construction of a temple in Jerusalem became his first priority. He dedicated himself and his nation's best resources to honor God with a spectacular building. Some 180,000 people worked to provide materials and construct the worship center. It took seven years to complete the temple, which was 180 feet long, 90 feet wide, and 50 feet high at its ceiling. The highest point of the structure's exterior was about 20 stories, or over 200 feet. Solomon spared no expense in making the temple beautiful. He used the best lumber, the most precious metals, and the most talented craftsmen in the world. His attitude seemed to be "Nothing but the best for God."

The Richest Ruler in the World (1 Kings 9–10)

Solomon soon became the richest king in the world—as well as the most powerful. He brought in vast riches and treasures from other regions. Some have estimated that Solomon was worth more than two trillion dollars in today's money.

As a nation, Israel was flying high during Solomon's reign. But the good times didn't last long. Solomon had been promised that his kingdom would last forever, as long as he followed God like his father David had. God warned Solomon not to turn away—otherwise, terrible things would happen (1 Kings 9:6–9). Sadly, Solomon did eventually fail.

Why Is There So Much Duplication in the Old Testament's Historical Books?

The books of 1 Kings and 2 Kings and 1 Chronicles and 2 Chronicles contain a lot of overlapping information. First Chronicles gives a detailed picture of King David's reign over Israel and ends with Solomon, David's son, taking the throne after his father's death. Second Chronicles covers more than four hundred years of history, beginning with the construction of Solomon's temple and ending with the Persian king Cyrus' proclamation that the Jews could return home to Jerusalem to rebuild the temple following seventy years of captivity that began under Babylon.

Ancient Jewish tradition says the priest Ezra, one of three key leaders to leave Babylon for the reconstruction of Jerusalem, wrote Chronicles after the captivity. Ezra repeated much of what was in the books of Kings to teach those who had returned from Persia how to worship God.

What are the differences? While the books of Kings focus mostly on historical events, 1 and 2 Chronicles emphasize the spiritual side of those events.

Solomon Goes Wrong (1 Kings 11:1–10)

Solomon's reign as king of Israel started well, but in later years he broke several of God's laws. He married *seven hundred* women. Solomon also had concubines, women who acted as wives though he had not married them (1 Kings 11:3). Among Solomon's wives were foreign women—Moabites, Ammonites, Edomites, Sidonians, and Hittites—who worshipped false gods instead of the true God of Israel. Over time, Solomon began building shrines for their fake gods.

God Pronounces Judgment for Solomon's Sin (1 Kings 11:11–13)

Solomon's foolishness angered God. One day, the Lord appeared to Solomon and told him that the great kingdom of Israel would pay a heavy price for its king's sin: "Because you have done this, and you have not kept My covenant and My statutes, which I have commanded you, I will surely tear the kingdom from you and will give it to your servant. However, I will not do it in your days, for your father David's sake. But I will tear it out of the hand of your son. However, I will not tear away all of the kingdom, but will give one tribe to your son for My servant David's sake, and for Jerusalem's sake, which I have chosen" (1 Kings 11:11–13).

Solomon's "Vanity"

The book of Ecclesiastes opens with these fatalistic words: "The words of the Preacher, the son of David, king in Jerusalem. 'Vanity of vanities,' says the Preacher. 'Vanity of vanities; all is vanity.' What profit does a man have from all his labor that he does under the sun?" (1:1–3).

Many scholars believe that Solomon—"the son of David"— wrote this book late in his life, reflecting on the emptiness of pursuing wealth, power, and pleasure to the exclusion of God.

If anyone understood that truth, it was Solomon. His career as Israel's third king began well, as he was fully committed to God and to His Word. But later, wealth and power—as well as a lust for women—took hold of his heart. The kingdom crumbled soon after his death.

Ecclesiastes shows us the meaninglessness of life—even a life of wealth and ease—when God is not our top priority. Most of the book is depressing, with no uplifting message from God. In the end, though, Solomon describes what he learned about the true purpose of life: "Fear God and keep His commandments, for this is the whole duty of man. For God shall bring every work into judgment, with every secret thing, whether it is good or evil" (12:13–14).

The Kingdom Divides (1 Kings 11–12)

In 1 Kings 11:31–35, the prophet Ahijah predicted that Israel would divide into two kingdoms. The split happened shortly after Solomon's death, as his son Rehoboam began to reign. Rehoboam foolishly refused to listen when leaders from northern Israel complained about the heavy burdens Solomon had imposed on the people (1 Kings 12:1–24). As a result, ten northern tribes broke away, becoming a new kingdom of Israel under the leadership of Jeroboam, a man who had served under Solomon. Rehoboam was king of a southern Jewish kingdom, Judah, reigning from about 931 to 913 BC.

Failed Leadership in the North and the South (1 Kings 12–14)

The northern kingdom of Israel fell into idolatry under Jeroboam's terrible leadership. The king was afraid that his people would travel to Jerusalem to worship God at the temple and perhaps lose their loyalty to him. So Jeroboam built two golden idols, one in Bethel and one in Dan—essentially the farthest northern and southern points of his kingdom. He told the people, "It is too much for you to go up to Jerusalem; behold your gods, O Israel, who brought you up out of the land of Egypt" (1 Kings 12:28).

Rehoboam also failed as a leader in the southern kingdom of Judah. His father, Solomon, had built a magnificent temple to honor God. But during Rehoboam's reign, the people angered God by following many false gods—and building altars for worshipping them. Some men added sexual immorality to their false worship (1 Kings 14:22–24). Rehoboam did nothing to bring his people back to the one true God.

Elijah

Elijah was one of the greatest prophets in Jewish history. He worked to lead the people of the northern kingdom of Israel away from Baal and back to the one true God. Elijah lived during the ninth century BC, after David and Solomon's Israel had split in two. Elijah performed many miracles, declaring a drought on the nation (1 Kings 17:1), raising a widow's son from the dead (1 Kings 17:17–24), and calling down fire from heaven (1 Kings 18:30–38), just to name a few. Elijah was enabled to perform these miracles so people could see he truly spoke for God.

That was obvious when Elijah challenged 450 prophets of the false god Baal at Mount Carmel (1 Kings 18:17–40). These false prophets called on Baal all day long, begging him (unsuccessfully) to send fire from heaven. Then Elijah built a stone altar, put an animal sacrifice on a pile of wood, and soaked everything with water. When he prayed, God sent fire from heaven to burn everything—the wood, the sacrifice, the altar, and the water around it. As God proved His superiority to Baal, Elijah and the true-hearted Israelites killed all the false prophets.

A New Prophet, Old Problems (2 Kings)

Second Kings opens with Elijah being taken to heaven in a chariot of fire. Then his assistant Elisha became Israel's leading prophet. The book also details the northern kingdom falling to the Assyrians around 722 BC (chapters 16–17) and the southern kingdom being conquered by the Babylonians around 585 BC (chapters 24–25). In between are the accounts of the various kings of Israel and Judah, most of whom served very poorly.

Where the Northern Kingdom Went Wrong (2 Kings 1–17)

Rulers of the northern kingdom of Israel were Jeroboam I, Nadab, Baasha, Elah, Zimri, Tibni, Omri, Ahab, Ahaziah, Joram (or Jehoram), Jehu, Jehoahaz, Joash, Jeroboam II, Zechariah, Shallum, Menahem, Pekahiah, Pekah, and Hoshea. None of Israel's kings followed God or encouraged His people to do so. One of the worst was Ahab, who led the people into worship of the false god Baal. Second Kings 17:7–17 provides a sad summary of the sins of the leaders and people of Israel, who worshipped false gods, practiced witchcraft, and "rejected [God's] statutes and His covenant that He made with their fathers" (2 Kings 17:15).

Elijah and Elisha

Elijah was one of two biblical people who never died. (The other was a man named Enoch, described in Genesis 5.) Elijah was taken to heaven in a "chariot of fire" on a whirlwind (2 Kings 2:11–12). Centuries later, when Jesus was "transfigured" before Peter, James, and John, Elijah appeared along with fellow Old Testament hero Moses (Matthew 17:1–4). Shortly before Elijah's departure for heaven, God instructed him to appoint Elisha as his successor. Elisha recognized the danger and difficulty of this job, so he made a special request of Elijah: "I ask, let a double portion of your spirit be upon me" (2 Kings 2:9). Elijah told Elisha that his request would be granted only if the younger man saw Elijah taken up to heaven. That event happened shortly afterward, with Elisha as a witness.

Like Elijah, Elisha was a powerful prophet of God who performed many miracles. In 2 Kings 2–13, well over a dozen miracles (including prophecies) are reported. Some examples: parting the waters of the Jordan River (2:14), providing water for the army of Israel (3:16–25), raising a boy from the dead (4:18–37), and curing the Syrian army commander Naaman of leprosy (5:1–19).

Israel Warned of Judgment (2 Kings, Prophetic Books)

God had repeatedly warned the people of Israel to turn away from their idolatry and back to Him. Elijah and Elisha both preached repentance to the people of the northern kingdom. Old Testament prophetic books Hosea (13:16) and Micah (1:6) foretold in writing the destruction of Samaria, the capital of the northern kingdom. Amos also accurately foretold the destruction of the northern kingdom of Israel, and Isaiah prophesied that God would use the Assyrian Empire to punish Israel for its idolatry (Isaiah 10:5–19).

The Northern Kingdom Invaded (2 Kings 15–18)

Beginning around 733 BC, the Assyrian king Tiglath-pileser invaded the northern region of Israel and took many people captive: "In the days of Pekah, king of Israel, Tiglath-pileser, king of Assyria, came and took Ijon and Abel-beth-maacah and Janoah and Kedesh and Hazor and Gilead and Galilee, all the land of Naphtali. And he carried them captive to Assyria" (2 Kings 15:29). In 721 BC, another Assyrian king, Shalmaneser, attacked Samaria, Israel's capital. Samaria fell three years later (2 Kings 18:9–12).

The Assyrians

Assyria was an ancient kingdom located between the Euphrates and Tigris rivers. From about 900–700 BC, Assyria was a powerful empire covering a huge area, with territory spanning modern-day Iraq, Syria, Jordan, and Lebanon. The Assyrians worshipped false gods and did terrible things to the people they conquered. Several Old Testament prophets spoke out against them.

The famous prophet Jonah was called to preach to Nineveh, capital city of Assyria (Jonah 1:1–3). Jonah initially refused God's assignment but, after a strange detour through the belly of a large fish, ultimately preached a message of warning to the city. When the king and his people repented, God turned His anger from Nineveh—at least for a time (Jonah 3:10).

In 701 BC, Assyrians attacked the southern Jewish kingdom of Judah. Led by King Sennacherib, the Assyrians took "all the fortified cities of Judah" (Isaiah 36:1) and then set their sights on Jerusalem. Hezekiah, a godly king in the fourteenth year of his reign, prayed for help—and God promised him that the Assyrians would never set foot inside the city (Isaiah 37:33). God killed 185,000 Assyrian forces in one night (Isaiah 37:36), and Sennacherib returned to Nineveh. There, his own sons killed him as he worshipped his god Nisroch (Isaiah 37:38).

Around 612 BC, an alliance of Medes, Babylonians, and Scythians attacked Nineveh, bringing an end to the Assyrian Empire.

The Southern Kingdom Continues
(2 Kings, 2 Chronicles)

The rulers of the southern Jewish kingdom of Judah were Rehoboam, Abijah, Asa, Jehoshaphat, Jehoram (or Joram), Ahaziah, Athaliah (the only ruling queen), Joash (or Jehoash), Amaziah, Uzziah (or Azariah), Jotham, Ahaz, Hezekiah, Manasseh, Amon, Josiah, Jehoahaz, Jehoiakim, Jehoiachin, and Zedekiah. While the leaders of the northern kingdom of Israel were all wicked men, Judah's kings had a slightly better track record. Of Judah's twenty monarchs, only about a third did well, and some of them made serious mistakes at some point in their reigns: Asa, Jehoshaphat, Joash, Amaziah, Uzziah, Jotham, Hezekiah, and Josiah.

Judah Declines (2 Kings, 2 Chronicles)

After the death of Josiah, Judah's last good king, Judah was ruled by a series of ungodly, wicked kings: Jehoahaz (609 BC), Jehoiakim (609–597 BC), Jehoiachin (597 BC), and Zedekiah (597–586 BC). None of these men loved or served God, and under their leadership the people of the southern kingdom fell further and further into idolatry and disobedience.

Though God sent several prophets to warn the people of Judah to turn from their idolatry and rebellion, they didn't listen. As a result, God would send judgment on Judah several decades after the fall of Israel.

Hezekiah

Hezekiah was the thirteenth king of Judah. He began his reign at age twenty-five and ruled for twenty-nine years (about 715 to 686 BC). Hezekiah was the son of an evil king, Ahaz, but he was nothing like his father. Hezekiah was one of the few kings of Judah who served God consistently. He is considered the best king in Judah's history.

Hezekiah's story is found in 2 Kings 16:20–20:21 and 2 Chronicles 28:27–32:33. One particularly interesting aspect of his life concerns a miraculous healing. At age thirty-nine, King Hezekiah became so ill that the prophet Isaiah told him to prepare to die. But instead of waiting for death, Hezekiah asked for God's mercy to live longer. Before Isaiah had even left the palace, God told him to tell the king that his prayers had been heard. Hezekiah was given another fifteen years of life (2 Kings 20:1–11).

Hezekiah stands out among all the leaders of God's people. He "did what was right in the sight of the LORD, according to all that his father David had done" (2 Chronicles 29:2). Hezekiah "trusted in the LORD God of Israel, so that after him there was none like him among all the kings of Judah, nor any who were before him" (2 Kings 18:5).

Prophets Warn of Judgment on Judah (2 Chronicles 35–36, Jeremiah, Etc.)

God sent many prophets to warn the people of Judah that judgment was coming. One of the "major prophets" (so named for the length of their books), Jeremiah shared largely bad news. God had given the people warning after warning through earlier prophets, but they hadn't listened. Now, destruction was coming. Jeremiah, who had faithfully carried God's message and suffered at the people's hands, would witness the utter destruction of Jerusalem.

God also spoke to Judah through the prophets Isaiah, Joel, Micah, Habakkuk, and Zephaniah.

The Fall of Judah (2 Kings 24–25, 2 Chronicles 36)

After warning Judah for so many years to turn away from idolatry and back to Him, God finally ran out of patience. He sent the Babylonian Empire to exact judgment on His people. The Babylonians came against Judah and Jerusalem in three different waves. In the first (around 607 BC), they captured many of Judah's bright young people (including a man named Daniel) and carted them back to Babylon. The second wave (598–597 BC) included the capture of King Jehoiachin, who was also taken away to Babylon. The third wave (around 586 BC) destroyed Jerusalem and its walls, razed the temple to the ground, and removed all the temple's treasures back to Babylon (2 Kings 24:13).

How Could God Use Evil People to Accomplish His Plans?

The Old Testament prophet Habakkuk understood that God had to punish Judah for its wickedness and rebellion. As God's spokesman, Habakkuk knew that the Chaldeans (or Babylonians) would soon attack and destroy Jerusalem. What he couldn't grasp was why God would use such wicked people to accomplish His purpose or will.

As the sovereign creator and keeper of the universe, God can and will do as He pleases. He has the right and power to choose whatever methods He wants to accomplish His will. God used the vicious Assyrians to judge the northern kingdom of Israel. Later He used the pagan Babylonians to punish the southern kingdom of Judah.

Habakkuk's reaction (1:12–13) shows us that God doesn't take offense when His people ask Him what He is doing. But we must always remember two things: (1) He's God and we're not, and (2) He doesn't owe us an answer. As the all-powerful and all-knowing God, He has everything under control, even if we can't fathom His ways.

MAIN ROAD

Jerusalem after the Babylonian Attacks
(Jeremiah, Lamentations)

The prophet Jeremiah had spoken God's warnings to Judah, and he knew the aftermath of the Babylonian attacks would be horrific. What he saw broke his heart, and Jeremiah recorded his account of the destruction in what became the book of Lamentations. He knew that the devastation was the result of the people's sin and rebellion: "The LORD has done what He had devised; He has fulfilled His word that He had commanded in the days of old. He has thrown down and has not pitied. And He has made your enemy rejoice over you. He has set up the horn of your adversaries" (Lamentations 2:17). The book of Lamentations shows why Jeremiah is often called the "Weeping Prophet."

Hope despite the Destruction
(Jeremiah, Lamentations)

You won't find a happy ending in Lamentations. But that doesn't mean all hope was lost. Jeremiah had prophesied horrific destruction as a result of Judah's sin and rebellion, but he also recorded these words of hope and restoration: "Behold, I will bring it healing and a cure, and I will cure them and will reveal to them the abundance of peace and truth. And I will cause the captives of Judah and the captives of Israel to return, and will build them as at the first. And I will cleanse them from all their iniquity by which they have sinned against Me, and I will pardon all their iniquities by which they have sinned and by which they have transgressed against Me" (Jeremiah 33:6–8). Jeremiah knew that Judah would be restored, and he knew that God would do that work after seventy years of captivity (Jeremiah 25:11).

Nebuchadnezzar

Nebuchadnezzar was king of Babylon from around 605 to 562 BC. Under him, the Babylonian Empire became one of the most powerful kingdoms in the world.

Babylon was located on the banks of the Euphrates River in modern-day Iraq. During Nebuchadnezzar's reign, Babylon was filled with impressive buildings and art. The king was an energetic builder with a clear vision of how he wanted Babylon to look. The king built "hanging gardens" for his wife, Amytis of Media. These gardens were one of the "seven wonders of the ancient world."

In biblical history, Nebuchadnezzar is best known for conquering Judah, then later destroying Jerusalem. He and his general, Nebuzaradan, destroyed the temple and most of the city, deporting many of the remaining residents to Babylon.

Daniel 3 says Nebuchadnezzar built a golden statue, presumably of himself, and ordered all people to bow down to it whenever music was played. In chapter 4, Daniel interpreted a dream for Nebuchadnezzar, telling the king that he should humble himself. Nebuchadnezzar disregarded the warning and was driven insane for seven years.

When he returned to sanity, Nebuchadnezzar declared of Daniel's God, "How great are His signs! And how mighty are His wonders! His kingdom is an everlasting kingdom, and His authority is from generation to generation" (Daniel 4:3).

Jewish Life in Babylon (Jeremiah 29)

In their three attacks, the Babylonians took many thousands of Judah's most gifted people to Babylon. There, they were treated fairly well. The Jews lived in towns and villages along the Chebar River and were allowed to raise their families, farm, and make a living. Jeremiah had encouraged the people to marry, have children, and build homes while they lived in Babylon.

The Fall of the Babylonian Empire (Daniel 5)

Babylon is the setting for the prophetic ministry of Daniel and Ezekiel, who were both imported from Jerusalem when Nebuchadnezzar's forces attacked Judah. Daniel prospered in Babylon, where he became an advisor to the Babylonian Empire and later the Persian empire.

Daniel 2 recounts the prophet's interpretation of King Nebuchadnezzar's dream, in which Daniel explained the downfall of Babylon. He further prophesied of the fall of the Babylonian Empire to the Medes and the Persians in chapter 5. The prophet Isaiah had also foretold the fall of Babylon (chapters 13–14, 21).

In 539 BC, less than a century after the founding of the Babylonian Empire, the Persian king Cyrus the Great conquered Babylon.

God's Prophets in Babylon

Ezekiel was one of the many people carried off to Babylon after the invasion of Jerusalem. Though the people of Judah were now living in captivity, Ezekiel preached of God's promise to one day restore their nation. Yes, God had judged the people of Judah, but He would also forgive them and bring them back to their homeland.

Daniel also lived during the captivity, having been brought to Babylon as a young man. Though he lived and served among people who didn't know God, he remained faithful, recording his prophecies and experiences while longing for his homeland of Judah. Daniel wrote, "In the first year of Darius, the son of Ahasuerus, from the descendants of the Medes, who was made king over the realm of the Chaldeans—in the first year of his reign, I, Daniel, understood by the books the number of the years, of which the word of the LORD came to Jeremiah the prophet, that He would complete seventy years in the desolations of Jerusalem" (Daniel 9:1–2).

God Fulfills His Promise (Ezra 1)

Though the book of Ezra is placed much earlier in the Bible than the books of the prophets, the events occurred around the same time. Ezra shows how God fulfilled His promise to bring the Jews back to their homeland after seventy years of captivity. The Lord used a series of surprising events to do so. Ezra opens with what is called "the Edict of Cyrus," known as Cyrus the Great, who was king of Persia. (Recall that, around 539 BC, the Babylonian empire fell to the armies of Persia.) In this expanded Persian Empire, Cyrus issued an order allowing the Jews to return to Judah. For his kindness and respect toward them, Cyrus is respected by Jews to this day.

Three Waves of Returnees (Ezra, Nehemiah)

After Cyrus' order, three waves of former captives traveled nine hundred miles from Babylon to Judah. The first wave was led by Zerubbabel. After settling in and rebuilding the altar so sacrifices to God could be restored, these Jews began building the foundation for a new temple. Some eighty years later, around 458 BC, the priest Ezra led a second wave of Jews to Jerusalem. When his group arrived, they began to restore the religious practices of God's people. Then around 445 BC, Nehemiah led the third wave of Jews to Jerusalem. Their primary task was to rebuild the walls of the city.

Esther

Esther was a beautiful young Jewish girl who lived in Persia, along with an estimated million other Jews, during the time of the return to Jerusalem, probably between the first and second waves. Esther was the wife of King Ahasuerus (called Xerxes in some Bible translations), making her queen of Persia.

When Esther's cousin and foster father Mordecai informed her of a plot to murder every Jew living in Persia, she risked her life to save them. Esther went to her husband, the king, without first being summoned, an action that could be punished by death (Esther 4:11). Ahasuerus was happy to see her and promised her whatever she asked of him. In the end, he allowed the Jews to turn the tables on their enemies, who were led by a selfish, prideful court official named Haman.

Esther's story, which is situated just before the book of Job in the Bible, is unique in that it never mentions God. Even so, He's clearly a big part of the story, working behind the scenes to save His people and continue their mission to bless the whole world.

Finishing the Temple (Haggai, Zechariah)

Though many Jews had returned to Jerusalem, they were slow to build a new temple to replace the one the Babylonians had destroyed years before. They laid a foundation and then stopped, troubled by the opposition of enemies.

Through the prophet Haggai, God declared, "These people say, 'The time has not come, the time that the LORD's house should be rebuilt." . . . Is it time for you yourselves to dwell in your paneled houses and this house to remain desolate?" (Haggai 1:2, 4). The prophet Zechariah carried this message from the Lord: "Let your hands be strong, you who hear in these days these words by the mouth of the prophets, which were on the day that the foundation of the house of the LORD of hosts was laid that the temple might be built" (Zechariah 8:9).

Prompted by the prophets, the governor Zerubbabel resumed the work, and this second temple was completed in about four years, in 516 BC.

God's Final Old Testament Words (Malachi)

The book of Malachi was written for the Jews in Jerusalem about a hundred years after the Babylonian captivity. The people thought they were pleasing God, but their hearts were far from Him, and God demanded they correct their attitudes. Malachi closed out the Old Testament; there would be four hundred years of silence from God, when He chose not to speak through any prophets. This silence was broken when John the Baptist proclaimed the Messiah's arrival, and the New Testament era began.

"Oddball" Prophets

The Old Testament includes three prophetic books not addressed to Israel or Judah. One, the very short book of Obadiah, pronounces judgment on Edom for fighting against Israel and gloating over its sufferings.

The second, the book of Jonah, tells of a wayward prophet who ran from God when he was called to preach to the wicked city of Nineveh. During his attempted escape, Jonah was thrown off his ship during a violent storm and swallowed by a giant fish. He came to his senses, prayed, and God had the fish spit Jonah onto the shore; then he went to Nineveh and warned the people of God's coming judgment. Everyone, including the king of Nineveh, repented, and God spared the city. . .at least for a time.

The book of Nahum, written around 150 years after Jonah's visit to Nineveh, pronounces a new judgment on the city. Nahum reveals that the Assyrians had forgotten the kindness and mercy God showed them in Jonah's day. They were filled with pride, violence, and idolatry, even worse than they had been before. "Woe to the bloody city!" God cried (Nahum 3:1).

5. THE MESSIAH:
Jesus' Life and Teaching, Death and Resurrection

MAIN ROAD -

The Old Testament Hints of the Messiah (Genesis 3:17)

You won't find the name of Jesus in the Old Testament, but the Jewish Bible really is all about Him. It tells the story of God working throughout human history to prepare the world for its Messiah. As the Son of God, Jesus lived in heaven in perfect harmony with the Father and the Holy Spirit (the three together comprising "the Trinity") for all eternity past. But after Adam and Eve brought sin and death into the world by their disobedience in Eden, God gave the first hint of His plan of salvation. The Lord told the tempter Satan, who appeared in Eden in the form of a serpent, "I will put enmity between you and the woman, and between your offspring and her offspring; He shall bruise your head, and you shall bruise His heel" (Genesis 3:15).

The Old Testament Predicts the Messiah (Psalms, Prophets)

Through the recorded history of God's chosen people, the Lord spoke through many men to give the Jews promises of a coming Messiah. The Old Testament includes predictions—all of which were fulfilled in Jesus—concerning the Messiah's virgin birth (Isaiah 7:14), where He would be born (Micah 5:2), that He would teach in parables (Psalm 78:1–2), that He would perform healings and other miracles (Isaiah 35:5–6), that He would suffer and die for His people (Isaiah 53), that He would be raised from the dead (Psalm 118:17–18), and many others. Some scholars count more than three hundred predictions about Jesus in the Old Testament.

Isaiah—the "Fifth Gospel"

The first four books of the New Testament—Matthew, Mark, Luke, and John—contain the story of Jesus' life. Together, they are called the "*Gospels*," a word meaning "good news."

But the Old Testament book of Isaiah, written around seven hundred years before Jesus' birth, contains so many prophecies of the coming Messiah that some Christians have called it the "fifth Gospel." Almost one-third of Isaiah's sixty-six chapters contain prophecies about the birth, life, and death of Jesus Christ, or about His return to earth in the end times. In fact, Isaiah provides more detail about the second coming than any other Old Testament prophet.

Isaiah's first "messianic prophecy" is that Jesus would be born to a virgin and would be called *Immanuel* (Isaiah 7:14). Matthew 1:23 provides a translation: "God with us." Isaiah's best-known prophecy, perhaps, says Jesus "was wounded for our transgressions, He was bruised for our iniquities. The chastisement of our peace was on Him, and with His lashes we are healed. We all like sheep have gone astray. We have turned, each one, to his own way, and the LORD has laid the iniquity of us all on Him" (53:5–6).

Isaiah 56 indicates that God's salvation through Jesus wouldn't be just for Israelites but also for non-Jews: "The Lord GOD, who gathers the outcasts of Israel, says, 'I will still gather others to them, besides those who are gathered to them'" (verse 8). That prophecy began to be fulfilled when Jesus' apostles—including Peter and Paul—began to preach to the Gentiles.

The "Annunciation" of Jesus' Conception (Luke 1:26–38)

Of the four Gospels, only Matthew and Luke say anything about Jesus' arrival into this world. Matthew wrote that Jesus' mother, Mary, "was betrothed to Joseph, [and] before they came together, she was found with child from the Holy Spirit" (1:18). Luke gives more detail about the conception of Jesus, reporting that the angel Gabriel appeared to Mary, telling her that she would soon give birth to the Son of God. Mary, a virgin, asked the angel, "How shall this be, since I do not know a man?" (Luke 1:34). Gabriel explained that God would perform a miracle, causing Mary to become pregnant with the Son of God. This would fulfill Isaiah's prophecy, "Behold, a virgin shall conceive and bear a son and shall call His name Immanuel" (Isaiah 7:14).

Mary and Joseph Guided to Bethlehem (Luke 2:1–21)

Mary and Joseph lived in the town of Nazareth in Galilee, a northern region of Israel. But the village of Bethlehem, in the southern region of Judah, had been prophesied as the Savior's birthplace (Micah 5:2). God ensured Mary and Joseph were in Bethlehem when Jesus was born.

The Roman emperor Caesar Augustus had ordered all Jews in Israel to travel to the towns where their families originated to register their names in a census. Joseph was a descendant of David, who was born in Bethlehem, so he and Mary dutifully traveled there.

Many others were already there for the census, so the couple couldn't find a place to stay the night. Ultimately, they lodged in a stable (or perhaps a cave), a place where animals were kept, and that's where Jesus was born. After His birth, Mary and Joseph wrapped Jesus in swaddling cloths and laid Him in a manger—a food box for livestock.

Women in Jesus' Genealogy

The Gospels include two genealogies (essentially family trees) of Jesus Christ—Matthew 1:1–17 and Luke 3:23–38. Matthew mentions four Old Testament women who were part of Jesus' family line: Tamar (1:3), Rahab (1:5), Ruth (1:5), and "the wife of Uriah," Bathsheba (1:6). Two of these women (Rahab and Ruth) were not Israelites, and all four had messy lives. Yet God used them to bring Jesus into the world. The implication is that Jesus lived and died to save people of all races and backgrounds.

In Genesis, the Bible's first book, God showed Abraham the stars in the sky, saying, "Look now toward heaven and count the stars, if you are able to number them. . . . So shall your descendants be" (Genesis 15:5). God also told Abraham that "in you shall all families of the earth be blessed" (Genesis 12:3)—that is, because his family line would ultimately produce Jesus, the Messiah.

Angels Announce Jesus' Birth (Luke 2:8–20)

In a field outside Bethlehem were shepherds watching over their sheep. The night's stillness was broken when an angel of God appeared and announced Jesus' birth. God's glory shone around the shepherds, and they were terrified. But the angel told them, "Do not fear, for behold, I bring you good tidings of great joy, which shall be to all people. For to you is born this day in the city of David a Savior, who is Christ the Lord. And this shall be a sign to you: you shall find the baby wrapped in swaddling cloths, lying in a manger" (Luke 2:10–12). The shepherds hurried into town and found Mary and Joseph, with the baby Jesus lying in a manger, just as the angel had said.

Jesus' Life Is Threatened (Matthew 2)

Sometime after Jesus' birth, perhaps within two years, Jesus was visited by "wise men" bearing gifts. Also called magi, these men were from "the east," probably Persia (modern-day Iran), hundreds of miles away. Observers of the skies, they said, "We have seen His star in the East and have come to worship" the child "born King of the Jews" (Matthew 2:2).

Their visit troubled King Herod in Judea, who took the report of Jesus' birth as a threat to his own rule. After the wise men left Bethlehem, an angel spoke to Joseph at night, saying, "Arise, and take the young Child and His mother, and flee into Egypt, and stay there until I bring you word, for Herod will seek the young Child to destroy Him" (Matthew 2:13).

Joseph obeyed immediately, and he and his family stayed in Egypt until Herod's death. This fulfilled another Old Testament prophecy: "Out of Egypt I have called My Son" (Matthew 2:15; see also Hosea 11:1).

Jesus' Childhood

The Bible reveals little about Jesus' childhood, except for a few quick glimpses: His circumcision and His presentation at the Jerusalem temple (Luke 2:21–40), the wise men's visit (Matthew 2:1–12), and His journey to Egypt and back (Matthew 2:13–23), all in His baby and toddler years, as well as His visit to the temple on Passover at age twelve (Luke 2:41–52).

At Jesus' dedication, a godly man named Simeon met Jesus, Mary, and Joseph. The Lord had promised Simeon that he would meet the Messiah; the day Jesus was presented according to the Old Testament law, the Holy Spirit led Simeon to the family. When he saw Mary and Joseph entering the temple with the baby Jesus, the Spirit told Simeon that this was the Savior he had been longing for (Luke 2:25–35).

Jesus attended His first Passover in Jerusalem at age twelve and immediately afterward demonstrated His uniqueness (Luke 2:41–51). As His family began their journey back to Nazareth, Jesus separated from them. Mary and Joseph searched frantically for three days, ultimately finding Jesus at the temple, discussing the law with Jewish teachers. Luke 2:47 says that "all who heard Him were astonished at His understanding and answers."

John the Baptist Prepares Jesus' Way (John 1:15–37)

John the Baptist was the first prophet sent by God since Malachi, about four hundred years earlier. John "came as a witness, to bear witness of the Light [Jesus], that through him all men might believe. He was not that Light but was sent to bear witness of that Light" (John 1:7–8). John preached of the coming Messiah and called people to repent of their sins.

One day, standing with two of his followers, John saw Jesus walking by. John immediately exclaimed, "Behold, the Lamb of God who takes away the sin of the world" (John 1:29). During Old Testament times, people had to sacrifice a pure, innocent animal such as a lamb to cover their sins. John's declaration indicated the purpose of Jesus' life on earth.

John Baptizes Jesus (Matthew 3:13–17)

Before Jesus began His public ministry, He traveled from Galilee south to the Jordan River, where John was baptizing those who had repented of their sins. Jesus never committed a sin but still asked John to baptize Him. "I have need to be baptized by You, and are You coming to me?" he said (Matthew 3:14). But Jesus insisted, telling John, "Allow it to be so now, for thus it becomes us to fulfill all righteousness" (Matthew 3:15). As Jesus came up out of the water, the Spirit of God descended on Him "like a dove," and a voice from heaven said, "This is My beloved Son, in whom I am well pleased" (Matthew 3:17).

John the Baptist: Miracle Baby

In the Old Testament, several babies were born under miraculous circumstances, including Isaac, Samson, and Samuel. In the New Testament, we find another miraculous birth—of a baby who would be known as John the Baptist.

He was born to elderly parents—a priest named Zechariah and his wife, Elizabeth, who had been unable to conceive. One day as Zechariah served in the temple, the angel Gabriel appeared and said, "Do not fear, Zechariah, for your prayer is heard. And your wife, Elizabeth, shall bear you a son, and you shall call his name John. And you shall have joy and gladness, and many shall rejoice at his birth. For he shall be great in the sight of the Lord, and shall drink neither wine nor strong drink. And he shall be filled with the Holy Spirit, even from his mother's womb. And he shall turn many of the children of Israel to the Lord their God. And he shall go before Him in the spirit and power of Elijah, to turn the hearts of the fathers to the children, and the disobedient to the wisdom of the just, to make ready a people prepared for the Lord" (Luke 1:13–17).

Zechariah was incredulous, and he lost his voice for a time as punishment for his disbelief. But, just as Gabriel had promised, Elizabeth had a son—who was called John. About six months before Jesus began His ministry, John appeared on the scene to prepare people for the Messiah.

The Devil Tempts Jesus (Matthew 4:1–11, Luke 4:1–13)

Immediately after Jesus was baptized, the Holy Spirit led Him into the desert to be tempted by the devil. Jesus fasted and prayed for forty days and nights, and Matthew notes, "He was hungry" (4:2). The devil, hoping to derail the Messiah's mission, tempted Jesus to do three things: turn stones into bread, jump from the top of the temple and rely on angels to break His fall, and worship Satan in return for all the kingdoms of the world. Jesus responded to all of the devil's temptations by quoting scripture (see Matthew 4:4, 7, 10). After the third temptation, the devil fled.

Jesus Calls His Disciples (Matthew 4:19–26, Mark 1:16–20, Luke 5:1–11)

Immediately after Jesus defeated the devil's temptations, He began calling a group of twelve men to travel with and learn from Him. These men are called Jesus' "disciples" (learners), but over time they became known as "apostles" (sent ones). Jesus' plan was for the men to follow and learn from Him, then take His message of salvation to the world after He returned to heaven.

The twelve disciples were Peter and his brother Andrew, James and his brother John, Philip, Bartholomew (or Nathanael), Matthew, Thomas, James the son of Alphaeus, Simon the Zealot, Thaddaeus, and Judas Iscariot. When Jesus called Peter and Andrew, who were fishermen by trade, He said, "Follow Me, and I will make you fishers of men" (Matthew 4:19). This meant they would soon begin catching people for God.

SIDE ROAD

Why Would God Allow Jesus to Be Tempted?

Matthew 4:1 says, "Jesus was led up *by the Spirit* into the wilderness to be tempted by the devil" (emphasis added). This temptation was no chance occurrence but a divine appointment set up by God the Father.

But why would He allow His beloved Son to endure such an intense trial? The writer of Hebrews explains: "For we do not have a high priest who cannot be concerned with the feeling of our weaknesses, but was in all points tempted as we are, yet without sin" (4:15).

As the eternal God, Jesus took on human form so He could identify with His creation. Then He faced temptation so He could further sympathize with us, the people He came to rescue. And, by wielding the powerful weapon of scripture against the devil's attacks, He set an example for us.

Years later, the apostle Paul elaborated on the use of scripture in battling temptation. "Take the whole armor of God, that you may be able to withstand in the evil day," he wrote. "Above all, taking the shield of faith, with which you shall be able to quench all the fiery darts of the wicked. And take the helmet of salvation and the sword of the Spirit, which is the word of God" (Ephesians 6:13, 16–17).

The Sermon on the Mount (Matthew 5–7)

One day, Jesus taught a large crowd gathered by the Sea of Galilee near the small fishing town of Capernaum, which He had made His home. From the hillside, Jesus preached what is called the Sermon on the Mount. He began with a list of nine statements of blessing, which came to be known as the "Beatitudes." (The word *beatitude* is a Latin term meaning "blessed," "happy," or "fortunate.") From there, Jesus delivered tough but practical teaching on subjects such as the law, marriage and divorce, asking and receiving from God, charitable giving, prayer, judging others, false teaching, true faith, and other important topics.

The Sermon on the Plain (Luke 6:20–49)

The Gospel of Luke contains a passage that some believe is a different account of the Sermon on the Mount and others think is a separate "Sermon on the Plain" preached at a different time. Luke begins with a similar list of Beatitudes and follows with some words of Jesus that overlap with Matthew's account. But some scholars note that the lead-up to this sermon says Jesus "came *down* with them and *stood on the plain*" (Luke 6:17, emphasis added). Even if the two accounts are of different sermons, Jesus' main points are consistent.

The Lord's Prayer

During His Sermon on the Mount, Jesus gave a beautiful model for prayer, which came to be called "the Lord's Prayer":

> *"Our Father who is in heaven, hallowed be Your name.*
> *Your kingdom come. Your will be done on earth as it*
> *is in heaven.*
> *Give us this day our daily bread.*
> *And forgive us our debts, as we forgive our debtors.*
> *And do not lead us into temptation, but deliver us*
> *from evil.*
> *For Yours is the kingdom and the power and the glory*
> *forever. Amen."*
> MATTHEW 6:9–13

Many people memorize the Lord's Prayer and recite it word for word. Others believe it's more a template for how to pray. For example, *"Our Father who is in heaven, hallowed be Your name"* refers to speaking words of praise to God. *"Your kingdom come. Your will be done on earth as it is in heaven,"* speaks of praying in accordance with God's will.

Jesus' Ministry of Healing (Matthew 8)

The Gospels tell us Jesus healed all kinds of people—men, women, and children, Jews and Gentiles—of various problems and diseases. In Matthew 8 alone, Jesus cleansed a man with leprosy (verses 1–4), healed a Roman soldier's paralyzed servant (verses 5–13), cured Peter's mother-in-law of a fever (verses 14–15), removed evil spirits and sicknesses from many people (verses 16–17), and cast demons out of a man and into a herd of pigs (verses 28–33). Such accounts occur throughout the Gospels. Jesus said He performed such miracles so people could know that "the Father is in Me and I in Him" (John 10:38). His miracles also fulfilled Old Testament prophecies such as Isaiah 35:5–6: "Then the eyes of the blind shall be opened, and the ears of the deaf shall be unstopped. Then the lame man shall leap as a deer, and the tongue of the mute shall sing, for waters shall break out in the wilderness, and streams in the desert."

Jesus Shows His Power over Death (Luke 7–8, John 11)

While He was on earth, Jesus demonstrated His power and authority over the weather, evil spirits, disease, and even death. The Bible records the stories of three people brought back to life by Jesus. The first—as it appears in the Gospels—was the son of a widow who lived in the village of Nain (Luke 7:11–17). The second was the twelve–year-old daughter of a synagogue leader in Capernaum (Luke 8:40–56). The third was His friend Lazarus of Bethany, who had been in the grave for four days (John 11:1–44).

SIDE ROAD

Seven "I Ams" of Jesus

In the Gospel of John, Jesus makes seven "I am" statements that reveal who He really is:

- ▶ "I am the bread of life" (John 6:35).
- ▶ "I am the light of the world" (John 8:12).
- ▶ "I am the door of the sheep" (John 10:7).
- ▶ "I am the good shepherd" (John 10:11).
- ▶ "I am the resurrection and the life" (John 11:25).
- ▶ "I am the way, the truth, and the life" (John 14:6).
- ▶ "I am the true vine" (John 15:1).

On another occasion, Jesus used only the words "I am" in response to a question from antagonistic Jewish leaders. See more on page 110.

Jesus Feeds Five Thousand People (Matthew 14:31–21, Mark 6:30–44, Luke 9:10–17, John 6:1–14)

Jesus performed dozens of miracles, and one of the most famous was feeding several thousand people with five loaves of bread and two small fish. Huge crowds followed Jesus—some because they were interested in His teaching and others because they wanted food or healing.

On one occasion, as the day wound down, Jesus told His disciples that the crowd needed to eat. But instead of sending them away to find food for themselves, Jesus multiplied a small amount of food into enough for the mass of five thousand men—plus uncounted women and children. John's Gospel notes that "those men, when they had seen the miracle that Jesus did, said, 'This is truly that Prophet who should come into the world'" (6:14).

Jesus Calms a Storm (Matthew 14:22–35, Mark 6:45–53, John 6:15–21)

Jesus then told His disciples to get in their boat and cross the Sea of Galilee. He would stay behind to pray. As the disciples were crossing the water, a violent storm arose. Knowing that His followers were in danger, Jesus went to them. . .walking on the water! When Jesus reached the disciples, He called out, "Be of good cheer. It is I. Do not be afraid" (Mark 6:50). When He climbed into the boat, the wind immediately stopped. The Gospel writer Mark notes that the men were "greatly amazed" (6:51), even though they had just witnessed an equally stunning miracle with the feeding of the five thousand men.

Why Were the Disciples So Slow to Believe?

After Jesus had calmed the storm on the Sea of Galilee, the disciples didn't know what to think. Mark 6:52 says, "They did not consider the miracle of the loaves, for their hearts were hardened." That means they were not yet ready to grasp exactly who Jesus was—even though He was performing stunning miracles in their presence.

For many Jews, apparently Jesus' disciples included, the Messiah was to be a conquering king who would deliver Israel from its Roman rulers. In time, though, Jesus would patiently teach His followers that He as Messiah had actually come to save people from sin. As their hearts softened, they would begin to see Jesus as He truly was—the Son of God who would suffer and die for human sin, then rise again to prove His power over death. In the disciples' time, Jesus was conquering human hearts. In the end of time, He would return as a conquering King ready to rule everything.

Jesus Faces Religious Opposition (Matthew 9)

Many who witnessed Jesus' miracles were amazed and began following Him. But the Jewish religious leaders weren't so impressed. They accused Him of blasphemy when He claimed the authority to forgive sins (Matthew 9:3–6), and they said His ability to cast out evil spirits came from "the prince of the demons" (9:34). Much of the opposition to Jesus came from the Pharisees, Jewish religious leaders who specialized in Old Testament law. Because so many people were following Him, the Pharisees saw Him as a threat to their own prominence.

Jesus, a Friend of Sinners
(Matthew 9:9–13, 11:18–19; Mark 2:13–20)

The Pharisees criticized Jesus for spending time with sinners. They felt that many people—for example, tax collectors—weren't worthy of God's mercy. The Jews in Israel, especially the religious leadership, detested tax collectors because they worked for the Roman government. And some had gotten rich by cheating their fellow Jews. When Jesus called a tax collector named Matthew, he immediately left his booth and became a disciple. Soon, Jesus was dining at Matthew's home, along with other tax collectors and sinners. Jesus told the critical Pharisees, "Those who are healthy do not need a physician, but those who are sick. But go and learn what this means: 'I will have mercy and not sacrifice.' For I have come to call not the righteous but sinners to repentance" (Matthew 9:12–13). Matthew, the one-time tax collector, would go on to write the Gospel account that bears his name.

Were There Any Good Pharisees?

Even though most Pharisees hated Jesus, two—Nicodemus and Joseph of Arimathea—were exceptions. Nicodemus is best known for his late-night conversation with Jesus in John 3, when Jesus stated what some call the gospel in a nutshell: "For God so loved the world that He gave His only begotten Son, that whoever believes in Him should not perish but have everlasting life. For God did not send His Son into the world to condemn the world but that the world might be saved through Him" (John 3:16–17).

Joseph of Arimathea was with the Jewish religious leaders who had called for Jesus' crucifixion, yet he opposed the decision because he was a secret follower of Jesus (Luke 23:51).

After Jesus' crucifixion, both Nicodemus and Joseph made arrangements, at great personal cost, to bury His body.

Jesus Speaks in Parables (Luke 15)

Psalm 78:2 reads, "I will open my mouth in a parable; I will utter dark sayings of old." The Gospel writer Matthew took this as a prophecy of Jesus' ministry (Matthew 13:35). On many occasions, Jesus spoke very plainly. But at other times, He taught through parables, fictional stories that made important points about subjects such as God's love and mercy, obedience toward the Lord, forgiveness, the kingdom of heaven, and God's understanding of our hearts. Jesus told more than forty parables. Perhaps He knew that people remember important lessons more easily when they come in the form of stories. He may also have figured that those who truly loved and followed Him would listen closely to understand the parables' meanings.

Jesus Praises Then Scolds Peter
(Matthew 16:13–20, Mark 8:27–33)

One day, near the city of Caesarea Philippi, Jesus asked His disciples who people were saying He was. The twelve replied, "John the Baptist. But some say Elijah, and others, one of the prophets" (Mark 8:28). Then Jesus asked the all-important question: "But who do you say that I am?" Peter answered correctly, "You are the Christ" (Mark 8:29). Matthew reports that Jesus replied, "Blessed are you, Simon Bar-Jonah, for flesh and blood has not revealed it to you, but My Father who is in heaven" (Matthew 16:17). Just a short time later, though, Peter showed that he still had much understanding to gain. After Jesus told the disciples that He would suffer, die, and rise from the dead three days later, Peter tried to correct his Lord. Jesus responded, "Get behind Me, Satan! For you appreciate not the things that are of God but the things that are of men" (Mark 8:33).

Pride versus Humility

In what is called the "parable of the Pharisee and the tax collector" (Luke 18:9–14), Jesus contrasted the words and attitudes of two men who had gone to the temple to pray. When the powerful religious leader prayed, he boasted of his own piety, reminding God how he had lived a more righteous life than most—he even gave a tenth of all he earned. The Pharisee actually told God that he was better than the tax collector across the way.

The other man had a totally different approach. He wouldn't even lift his eyes toward heaven but simply pounded his chest, crying out, "God, be merciful to me, a sinner" (Luke 18:13).

One of those two men left the temple made right before God, Jesus said—and it wasn't the Pharisee. Jesus said, "Everyone who exalts himself shall be humbled, and he who humbles himself shall be exalted" (Luke 18:14).

In the decades after Jesus' death and resurrection, His half brother James would write in a letter to all believers, "God resists the proud but gives grace to the humble" (James 4:6).

Jesus Transfigured (Matthew 17:1–13, Mark 9:2–13, Luke 9:28–36)

Not long before Jesus was arrested, tried, and crucified, He took His three closest disciples—Peter, James, and John—up a mountainside to pray. While Jesus prayed, His appearance changed. His face shone and His clothing turned a dazzling white. Two Old Testament figures, men who had lived centuries earlier, appeared and talked with Jesus about the trials He would soon endure. Moses and Elijah were two of the most important men in Israel's history: the former gave God's laws to His people, and the latter was one of the nation's greatest prophets.

One of Jesus' twelve disciples, Philip, had once said to his friend Nathanael, "We have found Him of whom Moses in the Law, and the prophets, wrote, Jesus of Nazareth, the son of Joseph" (John 1:45). How right Philip was—Moses and Elijah both represented the Old Testament scriptures, which all point toward Jesus.

The Greatest Commandments (Matthew 22:15–40)

Jewish religious leaders often asked Jesus questions, hoping to make Him say something they could use against Him. One day, an expert in the law of Moses asked Jesus which was the most important commandment. Jesus replied, "'You shall love the Lord your God with all your heart, and with all your soul, and with all your mind.' This is the first and great commandment. And the second is like it: 'You shall love your neighbor as yourself.' On these two commandments hang all the Law and the Prophets" (Matthew 22:37–40). Jesus had neatly summarized the Ten Commandments, which break down into the way we approach God (commandments 1–4) and our fellow man (commandments 5–10).

An Eighth "I Am" of Jesus

As they often did, Jewish religious leaders threw questions at Jesus, hoping to trip Him up so they could accuse Him of breaking God's law. When Jesus said that the patriarch Abraham "rejoiced to see My day" (John 8:56), they were incredulous. "You are not yet fifty years old," they responded, "and have You seen Abraham?" (verse 57).

Then Jesus dropped a bombshell. "Truly, truly, I say to you," He told the religious leaders, "before Abraham was, I am" (John 8:58). They knew exactly what Jesus was saying, and they were furious. Since God had used the name "I AM" to identify Himself to Moses centuries earlier (Exodus 3:14), Jesus was claiming equality with God.

Jesus was much more than a great teacher or miracle worker. He was the Son of God, the second member of the Trinity, God Himself in the flesh. By using the phrase "I am," Jesus was saying that He has always existed and will always exist through eternity.

Jesus' Ultimate Mission (Luke 13:22–35)

Jesus had spent about three years traversing the land of Israel on foot. During that time, He delivered profound teaching, performed many miracles, taught His twelve disciples, and showed people what God's love really looks like. But Jesus had one ultimate mission on earth, and that was to die on a Roman cross to pay for humanity's sins. He knew very well what awaited Him during Passover week in Jerusalem: "I must walk today, and tomorrow, and the day following. For it cannot be that a prophet perishes outside Jerusalem" (Luke 13:33).

The "Triumphal Entry" (Matthew 21:1–11, Mark 11:1–11, Luke 19:28–44, John 12:12–19)

The Sunday before Jesus was arrested, tried, and crucified, He rode into Jerusalem on the back of a borrowed young donkey. This fulfilled a prophecy found in Zechariah 9:9: "Rejoice greatly, O daughter of Zion; shout, O daughter of Jerusalem. Behold, your King comes to you. He is just and has salvation, lowly, and riding on a donkey, and on a colt, the foal of a donkey." In the week before Passover, thousands of visitors were in Jerusalem to celebrate and worship God. As Jesus entered the city, people lined the roadway, spreading their coats and palm tree branches ahead of Him and crying out, "Blessed is the King who comes in the name of the Lord. Peace in heaven and glory in the highest" (Luke 19:36). This is one of a handful of events in the life of Jesus recorded in all four Gospels. Christians now call this event the Triumphal Entry, the first major event of "Passion Week."

"Passion Week"

Passion Week is recounted in Matthew 21–27, Mark 11–15, Luke 19–23, and John 12–19. The Gospels record several important events during this week: Jesus wept over Jerusalem, "cleansed" the temple of money changers a second time, and disputed with the Pharisees about His authority. Jesus continued His teaching in Jerusalem that week, including what is called the "Olivet Discourse," describing the end times and the signs of His second coming (Matthew 24:1–25:46, Mark 13:1–37, Luke 21:5–36). Jesus also met with His disciples for the Passover meal, an event known as the "Last Supper" (Matthew 26:17–30, Mark 14:12–26, Luke 22:7–38). After the Last Supper, Jesus led His disciples to the garden of Gethsemane to pray as He waited for what lay ahead for Him (Matthew 26:36–56, Mark 14:32–52, Luke 22:40–53, John 18:1–11). Then He was arrested and taken into custody. He would be interrogated by the chief priests, the Roman governor Pontius Pilate, and King Herod (Luke 22:54–23:25).

The Last Supper (Matthew 26:17–30, Mark 14:12–26, Luke 22:7–38)

On the night Jesus was arrested, He met with His disciples for a final Passover meal together. In these last hours with His beloved followers, Jesus ate a meal, instituted "the new covenant in My blood" (Luke 22:20), and prayed His "High Priestly Prayer" (John 17) to encourage and strengthen the men. He also taught the disciples an important lesson about love, humility, and servitude by washing their feet, a task usually performed by the lowest of servants (John 13:1–17). That night, Jesus also identified the disciple who would betray Him—Judas Iscariot—telling him, "What you do, do quickly" (John 13:27).

Jesus' Arrest and Trial (Matthew 26–27, Mark 14–15, Luke 22–23, John 18–19)

Jesus never sinned in any way. But the Jewish leadership hated Him because He claimed to be the Son of God—so they hatched a plan to have Him arrested and killed (Matthew 26:3–5). With the help of Judas Iscariot, who agreed to betray Jesus for thirty pieces of silver (Matthew 26:14–16), they seized Jesus in the garden of Gethsemane. He didn't resist, going along quietly to stand before His accusers: the Jewish religious leaders.

The chief priests, elders, and teachers of the law questioned Jesus, asking Him if He was the Messiah. Jesus broke His silence to say, "I am" (Mark 14:62). The accusers declared Jesus guilty of blasphemy and sentenced Him to death. They could not, however, execute a criminal, so they bound Jesus and led Him away to the Roman governor, Pontius Pilate. Pilate and the Roman-appointed ruler over Judea, Herod, would also question Jesus.

What Part Did Pilate Play in Jesus' Death?

Pontius Pilate was the Roman governor of Judea during Jesus' arrest, trial, and crucifixion—and the man who gave final approval for His crucifixion. Pilate was in office from about AD 26–36 and served under Emperor Tiberius. Though Pilate found Jesus "not guilty" and tried several times to save His life, he ultimately gave in to the crowd's demands and allowed Jesus to be executed.

Pilate had no quarrel with Jesus. After meeting with Him, Pilate told the religious leaders who wanted Jesus dead, "Having examined Him before you, I have found no fault in this man concerning those things of which you accuse Him" (Luke 23:14). Pilate went on to ask, "What evil has He done? I have found no cause for death in Him. I will therefore chastise Him and let Him go" (verse 22). But the crowd was insistent, and "Pilate gave sentence that it should be as they demanded" (verse 24). He handed Jesus over to be crucified.

Jesus Is Crucified (Matthew 27:2–56, Mark 15:33–41, Luke 23:27–56, John 1:16–36)

Before Jesus was put on the cross, Roman soldiers tortured and mocked Him. John 19:2–3 says the soldiers "wove a crown of thorns and put it on His head, and they put a purple robe on Him and said, 'Hail, King of the Jews!' And they struck Him with their hands." The crown of thorns was a painful way of mocking Jesus as the "King of the Jews" (John 18:33, 19:21).

Carrying His own wooden beam, Jesus was led away to a place called Golgotha (or Calvary), where Roman soldiers drove large nails through His wrists and ankles, fixing Him to the cross. Then He was lifted up for everyone to see. Jesus was crucified with a criminal on either side of Him. His first words from the cross were "Father, forgive them, for they do not know what they do" (Luke 23:34).

The Agonies of the Cross (Mark 15:29–30, Luke 23:35–39)

Jesus experienced unimaginable physical agony as He hung dying on the cross. But He also suffered the indignity of intense mockery from the crowd. Passersby took His earlier words out of context and shouted, "Ah! You who are going to destroy the temple and rebuild it in three days, save Yourself and come down from the cross!" (Mark 15:29–30). Jewish religious leaders scoffed, "He saved others; let Him save Himself if He is the Christ, the chosen of God" (Luke 23:35). Even the Roman soldiers mocked Jesus: "If You are the King of the Jews, save Yourself" (Luke 23:37). One of the criminals crucified beside Jesus picked up the mockery: "If You are Christ, save Yourself and us" (Luke 23:39).

Jesus' Last Words

The Gospels record seven statements that Jesus made while He hung on the cross:

- ▶ "Father, forgive them, for they do not know what they do" (Luke 23:34).
- ▶ To the repentant criminal hanging beside Him: "Truly I say to you, today you shall be with Me in paradise" (Luke 23:43).
- ▶ To His mother, Mary, and His disciple John: "Woman, behold, your son!"... "Behold, your mother!" (John 19:26–27).
- ▶ "My God, My God, why have You forsaken Me?" (Matthew 27:46, Mark 15:34).
- ▶ "I thirst" (John 19:28).
- ▶ "It is finished" (John 19:30).
- ▶ "Father, into Your hands I commend My spirit" (Luke 23:46).

Jesus' Death (Matthew 27:45–56, Mark 15:33–39, Luke 23:46–56, John 19:28–30)

Around noon of the day Jesus was crucified, a strange darkness covered the land. Later, Jesus cried out to God the Father, "Eli, Eli, lama sabachthani?"—which means, "My God, My God, why have You forsaken Me?" (Matthew 27:46). When the time came for Jesus to die, He cried out "It is finished" (John 19:30), and "Father, into Your hands I commend My spirit"; having said that, Jesus "gave up His spirit" (Luke 23:46). At the moment Jesus died, miraculous things happened. In one, "the veil of the temple was torn in two from the top to the bottom" (Matthew 27:51), a visual indication that a new way had been opened to God's presence.

The Burial of Jesus (Matthew 27:57–66, Mark 15:42–47, Luke 23:50–56, John 19:31–42)

After Jesus' death, Joseph of Arimathea, a Jewish religious leader but secret disciple of Christ, asked Pontius Pilate for permission to bury the Lord's body. Pilate consented, so Joseph and the Pharisee Nicodemus took Jesus' body off the cross and wrapped it in burial cloth, along with about seventy-five pounds of myrrh and aloes, in accordance with Jewish burial customs (John 19:39–40). Joseph placed Jesus in his own new tomb and rolled a stone in front of it. Two women who had followed Jesus witnessed the burial and then went home to prepare additional spices and perfumes for Jesus' body.

Joseph of Arimathea

Joseph was a member of the Jewish ruling council, or Sanhedrin, who risked his reputation by helping with the burial of Jesus Christ. This account is found in all four Gospels: Matthew 27:57–60, Mark 15:42–46, Luke 23:50–53, John 19:38–42. Joseph opposed the council's decision to try to get Jesus executed, because he was secretly a disciple himself (John 19:38).

After Jesus died on the cross, Joseph, along with Nicodemus, approached the Roman governor Pilate to request the body. They were granted custody of Jesus' body, which they then prepared for burial. Per Jewish custom, they wrapped the body in strips of linen mixed with myrrh and aloe.

Jesus was placed in Joseph's own tomb, located in a garden near the place of the crucifixion. Probably without knowing it, Joseph—a wealthy man—fulfilled an Old Testament prophecy regarding Jesus' burial: "He made His grave with the wicked and with the rich in His death because He had done no violence, nor was any deceit in His mouth" (Isaiah 53:9).

Jesus Rises from the Dead (Matthew 28:1–10, Mark 16:1–8, Luke 24:1–12, John 20:1–10)

In Matthew 20:18–19, Jesus told His disciples, "Behold, we are going up to Jerusalem, and the Son of Man shall be betrayed to the chief priests and to the scribes. And they shall condemn Him to death and shall deliver Him to the Gentiles to mock and to scourge and to crucify Him. And the third day He shall rise again."

Jesus' words echoed those of Old Testament prophecies stating that the Messiah would die but that He would come back from the dead (Psalm 16:9–11, 118:17–18). Though Jesus died a horrible death on the cross and then was placed in a tomb, He would soon keep His promise to be bodily raised from the grave.

The Empty Tomb (John 20:11–22)

The risen Jesus appeared first to a woman named Mary Magdalene. She was a dear follower of Jesus, from whom He had cast seven demons (Luke 8:2). Mary had gone to Jesus' tomb very early on the Sunday morning after His death, and she wept outside. When she looked inside the tomb, Mary saw two angels in white, sitting where Jesus' body had been. They asked why she was crying, and Mary answered, "Because they have taken away my Lord, and I do not know where they have laid Him" (John 20:13). When she turned away from the angels, she noticed a man standing nearby—it was Jesus, alive again, and He told her to go tell the other disciples what she had seen.

Why Does Jesus' Resurrection Matter?

The apostle Paul reasoned that "if Christ has not been raised, then our preaching is useless and your faith is also useless. . . . And if Christ has not been raised, your faith is useless, you are still in your sins" (1 Corinthians 15:14, 17).

Jesus' resurrection is proof of who He claimed to be. It shows that He can be trusted to keep His word in all things. If He had failed to keep the promise of His own resurrection, He would have been discarded as a false messiah. But because He lives, we know that He has conquered death—and those who follow Him will too.

Paul wrote confidently, "If you confess with your mouth the Lord Jesus and believe in your heart that God has raised Him from the dead, you shall be saved" (Romans 10:9).

The Risen Jesus Appears to Others (Numerous Passages)

Jesus' appearance to Mary Magdalene was not the only one He made before returning to heaven. He visited with a group of female followers (Matthew 28:9–10), Peter (Luke 24:34), two men on the road to Emmaus (Luke 24:13–32), all of the apostles except for Thomas (Luke 24:36–43, John 20:19–25), the apostles including Thomas (John 20:26–29), seven of His disciples on the shores of the Sea of Galilee (John 21:1–25), the disciples on a mountain in Galilee (Matthew 28:16–20, Mark 16:15–18), more than five hundred believers (1 Corinthians 15:6), His brother James (1 Corinthians 15:7), the apostles as He ate a meal with them (Acts 1:3–8, Luke 24:44–49), and His followers just prior to His ascension (Mark 16:19–20, Luke 24:50–53, Acts 1:9–12).

Jesus Restores Peter (John 21:15–25)

Peter was one of Jesus' closest friends among the twelve disciples. He was always the one to speak up, even when he shouldn't have, or to act when no one else would. Peter seemed unshakably devoted, so much so that he once drew a sword to defend Jesus. But when Jesus was on trial for His life, Peter denied even knowing Him—three times. Following the resurrection, though, Jesus went out of His way to restore Peter, letting him know that he was forgiven. Jesus spoke to Peter about what lay ahead for him, both in terms of his ministry and his own death.

The Great Commission

Matthew 28:16–20 and Mark 16:15–18 tell of a meeting between Jesus and His disciples on a mountain in Galilee. There, Jesus prepared them for His departure, and He gave them the assignment they would carry out after He returned to heaven. This was the Great Commission: "All power has been given to Me in heaven and on earth. Therefore go and teach all nations, baptizing them in the name of the Father and of the Son and of the Holy Spirit, teaching them to observe all the things that I have commanded you. And behold, I am with you always, even to the end of the world" (Matthew 28:18–20).

The disciples would do just as Jesus commanded them, and much of their work is described in the book of Acts. They would ultimately change the world for good, but first they would need the power Jesus had promised.

6. CHRISTIANITY:
The Birth and Growth of the Church

MAIN ROAD

Christianity Begins (Acts)

The book of Acts—also called "Acts of the Apostles"—is a historical account of the early church, beginning with Jesus' return to heaven. It tells of the first generation of Christians, especially the apostles, as they were empowered by God's gift of the Holy Spirit (Acts 2) to take the message of salvation to Jerusalem, Judea, Samaria, and the surrounding world. The book also describes how a man named Saul (later known as the apostle Paul) went from persecuting the church to becoming the greatest evangelist in history.

Jesus Returns to Heaven (Acts 1)

After Jesus was raised from the dead, He stayed on earth for forty days. During that period, He visited the apostles several times, proving to them that He really was alive and giving them His final teaching about the kingdom of God. From the village of Bethany, on the Mount of Olives, Jesus told His followers to stay in Jerusalem until God sent the Holy Spirit (Acts 1:4–5). Jesus promised them, "You shall receive power after the Holy Spirit has come on you, and you shall be witnesses to Me both in Jerusalem and in all Judea and in Samaria and to the farthest part of the earth" (Acts 1:8). After that, "He was taken up, and a cloud received Him out of their sight" (verse 9). After approximately thirty-three years on earth, Jesus had returned to His Father in heaven.

The Ascension

Jesus' disciples stood in awe, looking intently into the sky as they watched Jesus ascend back to heaven. But as they stared, two angels in white appeared on the scene and said to them, "Men of Galilee, why do you stand gazing up into heaven? This same Jesus, who has been taken up from you to heaven, shall so come in similar manner as you have seen Him go into heaven" (Acts 1:11).

The angels' message was two-fold: First, Jesus' followers shouldn't stand around. . .they should be preparing for the work Jesus had given them to do. Second, Jesus would one day return in very much the same way as He had departed. For now, though, the disciples should focus on the work Jesus had prepared—and would continually strengthen—them to do. The balance of Acts shows how they took this message to heart.

Jesus' Promise of the Holy Spirit (Acts 1)

During His time on earth, Jesus had promised His disciples that He would send them a "helper" after He died, was resurrected, and returned to heaven. Acts 1:4–5 recounts that just before Jesus' ascension, He commanded the disciples to stay in Jerusalem and wait for fulfillment of "the promise of the Father." In case there was any question what that might be, Jesus explained: "For truly John baptized with water, but you shall be baptized with the Holy Spirit not many days from now."

The disciples then returned from the Mount of Olives to Jerusalem, where they gathered in "an upper room" (Acts 1:13). They and other believers prayed and waited.

The Church's Birthday (Acts 2)

God kept Jesus' promise of sending the Holy Spirit on a Jewish holiday called Pentecost (Acts 2:1). Many Jews from around the world were in Jerusalem at the time, and they would witness what God was about to do. With the believers gathered in a house in Jerusalem, God sent the sound of violent wind and what appeared to be tongues of fire that came to rest on each one. These followers of Jesus began "speaking in tongues"—languages they didn't even know, but which the visitors to the city recognized as their own (verses 9–11). The early Christians had all been filled with God's Holy Spirit. This day of Pentecost heralded the new way God would interact with believers—by actually living inside them.

"Speaking in Tongues"

When the believers in Jerusalem received God's gift of the Holy Spirit on the day of Pentecost, they "began to speak with other tongues, as the Spirit gave them speech" (Acts 2:4). They received the ability to speak in languages they didn't know. The apostles began sharing the gospel message with the crowds, speaking to each person in his or her own language.

Witnesses of the event—people from all over the world—could hardly believe their ears. "Now when this was reported outside, the multitude came together and were confounded, because every man heard them speak in his own language. And they were all amazed and marveled, saying to one another, 'Behold, are not all these who speak Galileans? And how do we hear every man in our own tongue, in which we were born? Parthians and Medes and Elamites and the dwellers in Mesopotamia, and in Judea, and Cappadocia, in Pontus and Asia, Phrygia and Pamphylia, in Egypt and in the parts of Libya around Cyrene, and visitors from Rome, Jews and proselytes, Cretans and Arabs—we hear them speaking in our tongues the wonderful works of God'" (Acts 2:6–11).

Peter Preaches Powerfully (Acts 2:14–47)

Many of those who witnessed the event of the day of Pentecost were amazed, but some mocked what was happening. "These men are full of new wine," they said (Acts 2:13). But the apostle Peter—the same Peter who had only recently denied even knowing Jesus—was now filled with the awesome power of the Holy Spirit. He courageously preached one of the Bible's greatest sermons. Peter assured the people that the believers weren't drunk; rather, they had been filled with God's Spirit. Peter went on to preach with such power that about three thousand people came to faith in Jesus Christ (Acts 2:41).

The Church Thrives (Acts 3–4)

The new church—meaning the believers living in Jerusalem—grew very quickly, and its growth alarmed the Jewish religious leadership. After Peter and John healed a man born lame at the temple, Peter preached another powerful sermon, and thousands more came to faith in Jesus. Peter and John were arrested and brought before the religious leaders, who ordered them to stop preaching the name of Jesus. But Peter and John refused, saying, "Whether it is right in the sight of God to listen to you more than to God, you judge. For we cannot but speak the things that we have seen and heard" (Acts 4:19–20). After being threatened against speaking about Jesus, Peter and John were set free—and kept telling people about their Lord.

The First Christian Martyr

The church in Jerusalem was growing like wildfire, and that led to persecution of the apostles and other believers. The first Christian to lose his life for his faith was a man named Stephen, who was "full of faith and power" and who "did great wonders and miracles among the people" (Acts 6:8).

When Stephen spoke courageously to the Jewish high council in Jerusalem, condemning them for crucifying Jesus, the promised Messiah, they became furious—so much so that they threw rocks at Stephen until he died (Acts 7:54–60). As the first Christian martyr breathed his last, the Bible says a man named Saul looked on in approval.

Stephen's death touched off a huge wave of persecution against the church in Jerusalem. All the Christians except for the apostles fled the city, scattering throughout the regions of Judea and Samaria and preaching the gospel as they went.

The Church's Chief Opponent (Acts 8:1–4)

Saul, later called Paul, was a Pharisee who desperately tried to hinder the message of salvation through Jesus Christ. Saul "began destroying the church, entering into every house and dragging off men and women, committing them to prison" (Acts 8:3). He persecuted followers of Jesus "to the death" (Acts 22:4). Saul hated Christians and believed he was doing God's will when he had them imprisoned and killed. He hated the very name of Jesus (Acts 26:9) and believed that His followers were blaspheming the name of God. But that changed when Saul met Jesus in a very personal and spectacular way.

Jesus Calls Saul to Serve Him (Acts 9:1–9)

Saul had violently opposed Christians living in Jerusalem and beyond. One day, he was traveling to the city of Damascus (located in modern-day Syria) to arrest believers and bring them back to Jerusalem to be jailed. But then blinding light from heaven surrounded him. Saul fell to the ground, blinded. A voice from heaven asked, "Saul, Saul, why are you persecuting Me?" (Acts 9:4). Saul wasn't sure who was speaking to him, so the voice said, "I am Jesus, whom you are persecuting. It is hard for you to kick against the barbs. . . . Arise, and go into the city, and you shall be told what you must do" (Acts 9:5–6). Paul, still blinded from the heavenly light, got up and continued to Damascus—but now for a totally different reason.

Peter's Vision of Animals in a Sheet

God gave the apostle Peter a strange vision of a sheet being let down from heaven by its four corners, filled with all sorts of animals—including some the Old Testament law considered "unclean," or not fit to consume. A voice from heaven told Peter, "Rise, Peter; kill and eat" (Acts 10:13). As a good Jew, Peter refused. But the voice said, "What God has cleansed, do not call that common" (Acts 10:15). The vision was repeated three times. Peter didn't know what to make of it, but God used a Roman soldier to show him.

Cornelius was a centurion stationed in the city of Caesarea. He was, according to Luke, "a devout man and one who feared God with all his house, who gave many charitable gifts to the people and always prayed to God" (Acts 10:2). And he became one of the first Gentile (non-Jewish) people to become a Christian.

Since he was Roman, Jews didn't want to associate with him. But when God told Cornelius to meet with Peter, the Holy Spirit told Peter to accept Cornelius as a brother. Peter realized God was telling him that he should never see anyone—even Gentiles—as "common or unclean" (Acts 10:28). After that, many Gentiles became Christians (see Acts 10).

Saul Meets a Christian Brother (Acts 9:10–17)

When Saul arrived in Damascus, the Christians there were understandably wary. They all knew the terrible things he had done to believers in and around Jerusalem. In time, though, they welcomed him as a brother in Christ. Saul was helped by a man named Ananias, a Christian living in Damascus. God had told Ananias to greet Saul when he arrived in Damascus, but Ananias was confused. Wasn't Saul the one who had been persecuting Christians? But God told him, "Go your way, for he is a chosen vessel for Me, to bear My name before the Gentiles and kings and the children of Israel" (Acts 9:15). Then the Lord added, "I will show him how much he must suffer for My name's sake" (verse 16).

Saul Begins Serving (Acts 9:18–35)

At God's command, Ananias greeted Saul and prayed for him at the home of a man named Judas. Ananias laid his hands on Saul and told him what God had said to him. Saul received both his sight and the Holy Spirit (Acts 9:17). Then he was baptized (Acts 9:18). Saul began visiting the nearby synagogues, telling people about Jesus (Acts 9:20). Because of Saul's reputation, other Christians were at first skeptical and fearful (Acts 9:21).

Saul later traveled and spent time in Arabia, Damascus, Jerusalem, Syria, and his native Cilicia (Galatians 1:17–24). A respected Christian man named Barnabas enlisted Saul's help to teach believers in the church in Antioch (Acts 11:25–26).

"Christians"

Today, a follower of Jesus Christ is called a "Christian." The word appears first in the book of Acts, which says, "And the disciples were first called Christians in Antioch" (11:26). Antioch, about three hundred miles north of Jerusalem, was a hub of the early Christian church. It was from Antioch that Saul, soon known by the Latin name Paul, launched the first of three missionary journeys.

Toward the end of his life, Paul described his faith journey to Herod Agrippa II, as the apostle stood trial for stirring up riots with his preaching. (Agrippa II was the last of the "Herodian Dynasty," a family that included Herod the Great, who tried to kill baby Jesus, and Herod Agrippa I, who executed the apostle James.) Herod Agrippa II said to Paul, "You almost persuade me to become a Christian" (Acts 26:28).

The word *Christian*, which means "follower of Christ," caught on. Followers of Jesus have been known as Christians ever since.

Paul's First Missionary Journey (Acts 13–14)

In Antioch of Syria, a sort of headquarters for the early church, a group of godly "prophets and teachers" (Acts 13:1) were worshipping God and praying when the Holy Spirit spoke to them: "Separate Barnabas and Saul for Me for the work to which I have called them" (13:2). After that, the leaders laid their hands on the two men, officially sending them out to faraway places to tell people about Jesus.

During Paul's first journey, he and Barnabas traveled from Antioch to the seacoast city of Seleucia, then to the Mediterranean island of Cyprus. From there, they went to Pamphylia, in modern-day Turkey. From there it was north to the region of Galatia, to another city called Antioch (Antioch of Pisidia). Then, after a trip of six to nine months, they returned to Antioch of Syria.

Two More Journeys (Acts 15–21)

Paul's second journey is found in Acts 15–18, and the third in chapters 18–21. In his second journey, Paul's traveling companion was Silas. They preached and taught in many cities, staying in Corinth, in modern-day Greece, for about a year and a half. On his third journey, Paul again visited several cities, some of them for a second time. He stayed in Ephesus for over two years before sailing to Macedonia, a region north of Greece, then traveling by foot for a second visit to Corinth. From Corinth, it was back to Macedonia, including a stop in Philippi. Ultimately, he would return to Jerusalem, where he would be arrested and imprisoned.

The Jerusalem Council

At the end of their first missionary journey, Paul and Barnabas traveled to Jerusalem to meet with other Jewish believers and discuss the many non-Jewish converts joining the church. At first, the church was made up mostly of Jewish converts. In Acts 13–14, Paul and Barnabas had won many Gentiles to the faith. Questions arose whether Gentiles had to convert to Judaism before they became Christians and whether Gentiles needed to observe the law of Moses in order to be saved.

After much prayer and discussion, the Jerusalem council issued four "rules" by which Gentile Christians should live: "It seemed good to the Holy Spirit and to us to lay on you no greater burden than these necessary things: that you abstain from meat offered to idols, and from blood, and from things that have been strangled, and from fornication. If you keep yourselves from these, you shall do well. Farewell" (Acts 15:28–29).

Paul's Missionary Legacy (Acts, the Letters of Paul)

Starting about AD 47, Paul dedicated his life to traveling and preaching Jesus. During his missionary journeys, Paul traveled some ten thousand miles—many on foot—and preached the good news of salvation in Jesus to countless people. He founded at least fourteen churches (perhaps as many as twenty) and wrote many letters that instruct, challenge, and encourage Christians to this day as books of our Bible—including Romans, 1–2 Corinthians, Galatians, Ephesians, Philippians, and Colossians, among others. Paul also mentored several people who continued his ministry after he was gone.

The End of Paul's Story (Acts 21–28)

Many people came to faith in Jesus when Paul preached. But many others hated his message. Paul was beaten, imprisoned, and threatened because he wouldn't stop talking about Jesus. He ended his third missionary journey in Jerusalem, where he was arrested for preaching the name of Jesus. The Lord appeared to Paul in a vision and told him, "Be of good cheer, Paul. For as you have testified of Me in Jerusalem, so you must also bear witness in Rome" (Acts 23:11).

Paul was taken to a city called Caesarea, where he spent two years in custody. While on trial before the Roman governor Festus, Paul demanded his right to be tried by Caesar in Rome. "You have appealed to Caesar?" Festus said. "To Caesar you shall go" (Acts 25:12). Paul ultimately sailed for Rome, an adventurous trip that included a shipwreck and the miraculous protection of all 276 people aboard.

Acts ends with Paul living under house arrest in Rome. He was largely free to do as he pleased, so he boldly preached and taught his visitors about Jesus. Though his biblical story ends with Paul in his own rented home (Acts 28:30), certain church traditions say he was ultimately beheaded by Roman authorities.

What Are Epistles?

In scripture, the book of Acts is followed by twenty-one books that are actually letters (also called epistles) written to various churches or individuals. Most of these epistles were written by Paul. Though they were written to certain groups or individuals in a certain time and place, they all offer something of value to Christians today.

Paul wrote thirteen epistles that became part of the New Testament: Romans, 1–2 Corinthians, Galatians, Ephesians, Philippians, Colossians, 1–2 Thessalonians, 1–2 Timothy, Titus, and Philemon. All of these letters instruct, challenge, and encourage followers of Jesus.

The other New Testament letters are Hebrews (authorship unknown), James (by "James the Just," probably a half brother of Jesus), 1–2 Peter (by the apostle Peter), 1–3 John (by the apostle John), and Jude (by Jude, a brother of James, and probably another half brother of Jesus).

The Bible closes with the Revelation, which is the only New Testament book of prophecy.

7. THE END TIMES:
Jesus' Return and the Renewal of All Things

MAIN ROAD

The Promise of Jesus' Return
(Acts 1:10–11, Revelation)

As Jesus ascended back into heaven, the disciples watched in wonderment. Just then, two angels appeared to them, saying, "Men of Galilee, why do you stand gazing up into heaven? This same Jesus, who has been taken up from you to heaven, shall so come in similar manner as you have seen Him go into heaven" (Acts 1:11).

The Bible, in both the Old Testament and the New, has much to say about Jesus' return to earth and the end of time. All of the prophecies of His return declare that God has a clear plan in mind for rewarding His own, punishing His enemies, and restoring all things.

Jesus' Return as Conquering King (Revelation 19)

Jesus came to earth the first time as the suffering Servant. But when He returns, it will be as conquering King: "And I saw heaven opened, and behold, a white horse. And He who sat on him was called Faithful and True, and in righteousness He judges and makes war. His eyes were as a flame of fire, and on His head were many crowns. And He had a name written that no man knew but He Himself. And He was clothed with a garment dipped in blood, and His name is called The Word of God. And the armies that were in heaven, clothed in fine linen, white and clean, followed Him on white horses. And out of His mouth goes a sharp sword, that with it He should strike the nations. And He shall rule them with a rod of iron. And He treads the winepress of the fierceness and wrath of Almighty God. And He has a name written on His garment and on His thigh: King of Kings and Lord of Lords" (Revelation 19:11–16).

Jesus Describes His Return

The Bible repeatedly promises that Jesus will come back to this lost, hurting, sin-corrupted world to mete out justice and make all things right. Some of those promises came from the Lord's own mouth. For example, shortly before His crucifixion, He told His disciples:

> *"And then the sign of the Son of Man shall appear in heaven, and then all the tribes of the earth shall mourn, and they shall see the Son of Man coming in the clouds of heaven with power and great glory. And He shall send His angels with a great sound of a trumpet, and they shall gather together His elect from the four winds, from one end of heaven to the other."*
> MATTHEW 24:30–31

Another time, Jesus made this promise regarding His return: "And if I go and prepare a place for you, I will come again and receive you to Myself, that where I am, there you may be also" (John 14:3). That's a beautiful promise to everyone who has trusted Jesus for their salvation.

Signs of the Times (Matthew 24–25, Mark 13, Luke 21)

In Revelation 22:20, Jesus says, "Surely I come quickly." But shortly before He was arrested and crucified, Jesus told His followers, "Of that day and hour no man knows, no, not the angels of heaven, but My Father only" (Matthew 24:36).

Human beings can't say exactly when Jesus will come back, and He never intended us to. But we can read the "signs of the times"—those events that indicate His return is near. In His "Olivet Discourse" (Matthew 24–25, Mark 13, and Luke 21), Jesus identified nearly two dozen signs that His return is close. He encouraged Christians to watch and remain faithful.

The Rise of Antichrist (Revelation 13)

John recorded a disturbing end-times vision of two frightening beasts and a dragon (Satan). The first beast came out of the sea. It had seven heads and ten horns—each with a crown on top. Every horn contained some blasphemy against God. The second beast rose from the earth and had two horns like a lamb, though it spoke like a dragon. Many believe the first beast symbolizes a union of the nations of the world and the second symbolizes the Antichrist—the same evil person the apostle Paul called "[the] man of sin" and "the son of destruction" (2 Thessalonians 2:3). The Antichrist and his deeds are also described in Daniel 9:27 and 11:36–45.

666

Revelation 13:16–17 provides a chilling warning: "He causes all, both small and great, rich and poor, free and bond, to receive a mark on their right hand or on their foreheads, and that no man might buy or sell, except him who had the mark or the name of the beast, or the number of his name." This mark, often called "the mark of the Beast," is a seal for followers of the Antichrist and his false prophet. The false prophet causes people to take this mark.

The next verse continues, mysteriously: "Here is wisdom. Let him who has understanding count the number of the beast, for it is the number of a man, and his number is six hundred and sixty-six." Many theologians believe this number is a clue about the identity of the Antichrist, but the exact significance of the number 666 is unclear. Throughout history, some have used the number to try to identify the Antichrist as Emperor Nero, various Catholic popes, and even President Ronald Reagan.

The Great Tribulation (Revelation 7)

Revelation 7:14 mentions a "great tribulation." This is the terrible time in which God will judge the world. The Bible says it will last seven years. Opinions differ on where Christians will be during this time. Some believe Jesus will take His followers to heaven before the great tribulation, in an event called "the rapture." Others believe Christians will remain on earth for half of the tribulation. Still others believe Christians stay on earth the whole seven years.

The tribulation begins when the Antichrist comes into power and enters into a pact with the nation of Israel (Daniel 9:27). The period will include wars, famines, plagues, and natural disasters as God pours out His wrath against sin, evil, and godlessness on earth. According to the book of Revelation, the tribulation will include appearances of the four horsemen of the Apocalypse, and numerous judgments identified by seals, trumpets, and bowls in heaven.

Armageddon (Revelation 16)

In Revelation, the term *Armageddon* refers to a climactic future battle between God and the forces of evil. Revelation 16:16 introduces us to the word. In the Hebrew language, it means "Mount Megiddo." In this place, God will destroy the armies of the Antichrist, as many people from all nations will gather to fight against Jesus. With the Antichrist in command, the kings and leaders of earth will gather their forces for a massive assault on the city of Jerusalem. But Jesus will stand on the Mount of Olives (Zechariah 14:4) with the armies of heaven at His command. He will defeat the forces of evil once and for all (Revelation 19:15–16).

The Rapture

You won't find the word *rapture* in the Bible. It comes from a Latin word meaning "a carrying off" or "a snatching away." Many Christians believe that the rapture is a future event in which God takes His followers to heaven before He judges the earth. This idea comes from 1 Corinthians 15:50–54: "Now I say this, brothers, that flesh and blood cannot inherit the kingdom of God. Nor does corruption inherit incorruption. Behold, I tell you a mystery: We shall not all sleep, but we shall all be changed, in a moment, in the twinkling of an eye, at the last trumpet. For the trumpet shall sound, and the dead shall be raised incorruptible, and we shall be changed. For this corruptible must put on incorruption, and this mortal must put on immortality. So when this corruptible has put on incorruption and this mortal has put on immortality, then the saying that is written shall come to pass: 'Death is swallowed up in victory.'"

The apostle Paul, who wrote 1 Corinthians, made similar comments in his first letter to the Thessalonians: "But I do not want you to be ignorant, brothers, concerning those who are asleep, lest you sorrow as others who have no hope. For if we believe that Jesus died and rose again, even so God will bring with Him those who sleep in Jesus. For we say this to you by the word of the Lord, that we who are alive and remain until the coming of the Lord will not precede those who are asleep. For the Lord Himself shall descend from heaven with a shout, with the voice of the archangel, and with the trumpet of God. And the dead in Christ shall rise first. Then we who are alive and remain shall be caught up together with them in the clouds to meet the Lord in the air. And so we shall be with the Lord forever" (4:13–17).

Satan Is Defeated (Revelation 20)

The book of Revelation contains many disturbing—even terrifying—images. There are terrible predictions of what will happen on earth in the end times. But Revelation ends with an uplifting, encouraging message: God wins. And so do those who follow Him.

For thousands of years, Satan has worked death and destruction on humankind. He's had quite a run, but the Bible says that it will end. Revelation describes Satan's future: "And the devil, who deceived them, was cast into the lake of fire and brimstone, where the beast and the false prophet are, and shall be tormented day and night forever and ever" (Revelation 20:10).

The Universe Is Restored (Revelation 21–22)

Jesus once said, "Heaven and earth shall pass away, but My words shall not pass away" (Mark 13:31). Revelation 21 explains what will become of the old heaven and earth—and what will replace them: "And I saw a new heaven and a new earth, for the first heaven and the first earth had passed away, and there was no more sea. And I, John, saw the holy city, new Jerusalem, coming down out of heaven from God, prepared as a bride adorned for her husband" (verses 1–2). When this all happens, "God shall wipe away all tears from their eyes, and there shall be no more death or sorrow or crying, nor shall there be any more pain, for the former things have passed away" (verse 4). From that moment on, the curse of sin will be gone forever (Revelation 22:3), and a perfect eternity begins.

Another Great Bible Reference

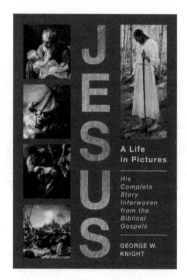

Curious about the life of Jesus? This beautiful book will help you visualize the people, places, and events surrounding His time on earth. Based on a blending of the four Gospel accounts in Barbour's fresh, new Simplified King James Version, *Jesus, a Life in Pictures* features full-color artwork throughout, plus informative maps at the end.

Paperback / 978-1-63609-239-3